There Was a Little Girl in the Corner

LINDA CARTER

Fulton Books
Meadville, PA

Published by Fulton Books 2021

ISBN 978-1-63710-388-3 (paperback)
ISBN 978-1-63710-389-0 (digital)

Printed in the United States of America

I would like to dedicate my story in memory of my beloved Mother, Maggie.

Mrs Carter

If you were to meet Mrs. Linda Carter today, you would have no idea of the turmoil that she experienced while growing up. Although her story is full of sadness, it also demonstrates an incredible strength that ultimately overcomes many obstacles. Mrs. Carter tells us about the strength of her mother, which continues to shine through Mrs. Carter today!! Sadness and stress swept through this family, yet was overcome through the strength of their faith in God. This story will inspire all who read it. I am absolutely awed by the details of her childhood memories right down to what her mother purchased for her first day of school. This is a story of strength, faith, and love. Her love for the LORD and music are nothing short of being inspirational. The story of how her trials helped her get through her most difficult times, and bring her out of the corner is a great read. It is truly amazing that the little girl in the corner grew up to become such a strong and loving individual.

Melissa Burgio

THERE WAS A LITTLE GIRL IN THE CORNER

Proverbs 18:22 declares "Who so findeth a wife, findeth a good thing, and obtaineth favour of the LORD." Mrs. Linda Diane Carter is a "Wife, and a Good Thing." It is imperative that each and every man understand that every woman isn't necessarily a WIFE, or even a woman. First, being a male is a matter of birth, but being a man is a matter of character. In like manner being a female is a matter of birth, but being a woman is a matter of character. The Woman and Wife that I love, and have been married to for going on forty five years is the "Virtuous Woman." The Bible indicates that the "Virtuous Woman" is indeed a rare find.[10] *Who can find a virtuous woman? for her price is far above rubies.[11] The heart of her husband doth safely trust in her, so that he shall have no need of spoil.[12] She will do him good and not evil all the days of her life. Prov 31:10-12 (KJV).*

I have boldly described my wife in this fashion because, in all of the years that we've been together, she has been nothing but good to me. Mrs. Carter is not only with me, but she is also for me. A person can be with you, but not necessarily for you. Of course it is necessary to understand that we didn't start out this way as is attested to in the book. But I must say that I have never regretted being married to Linda. When I initially met Linda both she and I were in pretty bad shape. At that time my life was seriously vexed with some major problems. I was just emerging from a situation where I

7

had been living my life as what I refer to as a "tumbleweed." I know that I was really looking for a "Wife," but was completely unable to find one. And so when I met Linda, I had just found my way out of a very unhealthy relationship. I was living in my mother's apartment, and, was earnestly looking for a job for about a year before finally finding one. During that period of my life I worked during the day, and spent my evenings sitting on the stoop smoking marijuana. My mother's apartment was located on Sterling Place between Bedford and Franklin Avenues in Brooklyn on the odd numbered side of the street. One evening as I was sitting on the stoop I noticed that the even numbered side of the street was completely dark except for one house that had this light shining in the window. As I sat there I became very curious about that light and who was living in that house. I became so curious that I found myself leaving my stoop and walking down the block to look across the street into that window, to see if anyone was there. However, I didn't see anyone. I met Linda Diane Hall somewhere around the Fourth of July, 1976 in a disco-theque called "The Last Word." I inquired if she would dance with me and she consented. We danced together, and we talked for quite some time. In fact, we talked to each other for about three hours. And while we were talking, we exchanged contact information with each other. Little did I realise that Lind Hall, the young lady that I met at The Last Word was the woman that lived in the house that had the light that I was so curious about. However, I also didn't real-ise the trouble that she was experiencing in her own life. As we con-tinued to interact with one another, I would discover that Linda had been the victim of several nervous breakdowns. By this time I had fallen in love with her and decided that although I was advised not to stay with her, I wouldn't leave her. I recognized that when people are doing well, we all want to be loved. But when people are going through some type of struggle, we need to be loved and supported. During the course of our relationship before and after marriage, Mrs. Carter would suffer breaking down every year for about five years. However, eventually the LORD would heal her completely. And the both of us would go on to salvation, and live a wonderful life with each other in the LORD Jesus Christ. As we continue together in the

8

LORD, Mrs. Carter has displayed and continues to develop all of the virtues and characteristics of the "Virtuous Woman." It is because of Mrs. Carter and the love demonstrated to me by her family that I eventually gave my life to the LORD Jesus Christ. Marrying my wife and giving my life to the LORD are the two best decisions that I have made in my entire life. Enjoy the book.

Have you ever felt like escaping from all of the dark secrets of your mind? This is what my story is all about. I could no longer handle all of the consequences of the sins that I had committed, nor of the sins that had been committed against me. Most of the time when one has experienced things that are too horrible to think of, they attempt to tuck the bad memories of those things in the corners of their minds. This is exactly what I did. I attempted to escape the horror of those memories by tucking them far away in the corners of my mind. That's where the little girl in me lived, and felt safe. I thought that I would hide in that corner for the rest of my life. However, in 1975 something so cataclysmic happened to me that it would ultimately change my life forever. This event eventually caused the little girl in the corner of my mind to finally and completely emerge. It took the genuine love of God, and many authentic prayers for my healing to be completed.

I thank God for the prayers of my mother, Mrs. Maggie Melissa Jones. The LORD used her and her prayer life to bring me out of the horrible dark past that I was too afraid to face. In 1975 my mother spoke these words to me when I experienced my first complete nervous breakdown. "It's going to take true love to bring you out of this." The words that she spoke were the absolute truth. In 1982, I received a miraculous healing and deliverance from my terrible dark past. Allow me to take you back to the very beginning of my life as that little girl in the corner.

In 1957 I remember my mother moving three of my four brothers, my sister, and myself from Portsmouth Virginia to the Bronx in New York City. I was only five years old. I remember riding through the Portsmouth Tunnel. It was lit with low yellow lights, and I remember the tunnel curving slightly as we were driving through it. I remember there was a strange gentleman driving. It was only after many years had passed in my life that I would learn that the man who was driving us was my father. I also recall us stopping at the Maryland House in order to go to the restroom, and to eat the fried chicken sandwiches and drinks that my mother had prepared for the trip. I remember the trip being so long that I kept falling in and out of sleep.

Finally, when we arrived, we went to 832 Dawson Street in the South Bronx, where I met this lady who was slightly hump-backed named Miss Mazy. Before moving us, my mother and Miss Mazy had arranged for us to stay in her three bedroom apartment with her. Two of my brothers, Vernon and David, stayed in upstairs bedroom with a man named Mr. Hardy. I would learn later on that my mother and father had separated from each other, and that was the reason why we moved to New York City. My eldest brother Aaron Hall Jr. stayed in Portsmouth with our Aunt Doll, my mother's youngest sister, and her husband, Uncle Bernie. I have always thought my mother to be a very brave woman to move all of us to a big strange city like New York. I would learn sometime later the reason why she left my father. He physically and emotionally abused her. So she felt that she had to get away from him. There is one main attribute that I have always admired about my mother. She loved her family and her children always came first in her life. I was born on August 30, 1952 in Kings Daughters Hospital in Portsmouth Virginia. Two of my brothers, Aaron, and Ronnie were born in our house in Virginia. And my grandmother Mrs. Daisy Moore assisted with their deliveries. I also had an older sister named Rosemary who died at the age of nine. This might sound ludacris, but I can remember my mother holding me in her arms at Rosemary's funeral. It is reported that Rosemary died of kidney failure. However my two oldest brothers would recall to me how Rosemary suffered a lot of physical abuse from my father.

I am extremely sorry that I never got to know her. But the odd thing is that I look very much like her, and both of us love(d) singing and making up songs.

In September of 1957 my mother registered me into school. The school wasn't too far from where we lived. I will never forget my first day of school. I started in kindergarten, and I remember Mom holding my hand as she escorted me to my classroom. I remember lining up against the wall outside of the classroom. I remember crying after my mother left me there. There was a caucassian boy with a round face and blond hair. I don't remember what he said to me, but I do recall slapping him across his face. And I remember watching his cute little face turn red. I really enjoyed going to school, and as far as I can remember, I never had to fight in school again. My mother bought both my sister Joyce and I two plaid dresses. Each of them came with crinoline slips. My mother supplied both of us with Monday through Sunday panties, socks, and one pair of shoes at the beginning of the school year. She would fix both of our hair with a ponytail and a big bang. In class we learned how to read the Dick and Jane books. I loved learning how to read and writing my alphabet. I was given the task of erasing and cleaning the blackboards in class, and I loved it.

Miss Mazy would watch over us while my mother would go to work all week as a live-in housekeeper for some people named Hathaway. My sister and I shared a small bedroom, and Ronnie slept in a bedroom that was located down a long hall. Miss Mazy was a very strange woman to me. I remember her staying up all night, and sorting little strips of paper with numbers on them. I believe that she was what was known as an illegal "numbers runner." This was one of the more common ways that people earned a living in the Black community. Miss Mazy was a cigarette smoker, and when she smoked, she would never flick the ashes from her cigarette. Sometimes I would catch her nodding off to sleep with a cigarette hanging from her lips, and her false teeth hanging halfway out of her mouth. As you probably can imagine, this was a very frightening sight to a five year old. When I had to I would quietly crawl under her chair to get to the bathroom that was down that long hall.

Every afternoon at 12 o'clock, Miss Mazy would pick me up from my kindergarten class and take me home. She would make me a sandwich and give me a glass of milk for my lunch. I could hardly wait for it to be Friday. That's when my mother came home from work. She always found some time to take us to the movies, or take us out on a picnic. On some Saturdays she would take us to Palisades Amusement Park in New Jersey. On Friday nights we would watch wrestling which really didn't interest me. I would go to my room and play with the toy baby doll that Mom had bought for me. A lot of times on Friday, one of my older brothers, Vernon would play a card game with us called "Knuckles." This game was played in a way that the person who had the most cards left in their hands after a hand was finished would suffer their little fisted knuckles to be hit with the whole stack of cards. How many times one was struck was determined by how many cards were left in their hands. Vernon always warned me and Ronnie before we played the game with him that he would have no pity on us when we lost the game. However, in spite of knowing the consequences of losing, we always chose to play the game with our brother.

Whenever my sister or brothers would take me, I would go outdoors to play. One day I met a girl whose name was Karen. Karen lived with her mother, grandmother, sister, and two brothers a few buildings down the block from me. We soon became the best of friends, and had a lot of fun together. During the summer we would play together all day. And as soon as either of us acquired a few nickels and dimes in our hands we were off to the corner store to buy candy, gum, and cookies. One day Karen and I decided to become "blood sisters." We got a sewing needle and both of us pricked our fingers and mixed our blood together. We loved to play Hopscotch, Softball, and Double Dutch. There was a center near a park on Prospect Avenue called "Sixty." We would go there to participate in after-school activities. At the center we were allowed to participate in arts and crafts, and play board hockey. Music was always being played throughout the center on its PX system. This is when the Motown recording label was the hottest one in the country. It had all of the top recording stars like Stevie Wonder, The Supremes, The

Temptations, Martha and the Vandellas, The Four Tops, and Smokey Robinson and the Miracles. The center would sponsor dances every Friday night, and my sister and I would go to them sometimes. One Friday we went to the dance, and from a distance, we saw this really handsome guy. He was so cute. As we approached the table where he was sitting we soon discovered that the guy we were falling all over was our brother Vernon. He had gone to the beauty parlor and had his natural hair permed into a Marcel. We were really embarrassed, to say the least.

Karen and I had so much fun growing up on Dawson Street. Sometimes we argued about minor stuff. But we would always make up, and go back to playing and discovering our world together. Unfortunately we didn't realize just how dangerous the block we lived on was. Back then we had no earthly idea of the dangers that we had been exposed to. We were unwittingly allowed to wander through our neighborhood completely oblivious to the 'lions, tigers, and bears' that were out there. Children as young as we were (and we were extremely young) should never have been allowed to see and go through what we saw and did. Home should always be a safe haven for little children. Children should never be allowed to aimlessly roam the neighborhood. Please don't misunderstand me. I truly appreciate the bravery of my mother raising her children alone, but there were many times that I longed for the protection of my father.

Fridays couldn't come soon enough. This was the day that Mother took us to the movies. The first movie that I remember seeing with my family was called "Tom Thumb." I can still recall the theme song. My mother was really into gospel music. And on some weekends she would take us into Harlem to the Apollo Theater to see some of her favorite gospel artists. One of my mother's favorite artists was Shirley Caesar and the Caravans. Mother told us stories of her singing with Miss Caesar when she was a younger woman living back in Portsmouth. Some time later I learned from my brothers that Mother loved singing, and even had my brothers and my sister Rosemary perform for a local television station in Portsmouth. My mother's love for singing gave me the inspiration to sing. It wasn't long before my mother started taking us to this Baptist Church.

The building was huge and had a very large auditorium, and an oval balcony. We were guided to our seats by older women who wore starched white uniform dresses. They were called ushers. They were positioned at the entrance doors of the building and also stood at the front ends of the pews. My mother met this wonderful lady there named Miss Beatie. Miss Beatie was the pianist for the church choirs. I believe the name of the congregation was called the Ebenezer Baptist Church and was located in the Bronx. On some Friday evenings, Miss Beatie would invite us over to her home where she lived with her husband who we very rarely saw. The first song that I remember singing was called "Swing Low Sweet Chariot." My youngest brother Ronnie and I would sing this song together. Although Ronnie didn't like to sing with me, I really loved singing. It was the one activity that always brought me complete peace of mind. I believe that my mother thought me to be too young to be baptized, because she allowed Joyce to be baptized, but didn't allow baptism for me.

Later that year, in 1957 my mother sent for my eldest brother Aaron Jr. to come to New York. At the time I thought that Aaron didn't want to come to New York, but I found out much later that he did. I didn't remember knowing Aaron when we lived in Portsmouth. When he arrived it was as if I had met him for the first time, but he knew me well. After all, he was eight years older than I was. Aaron was thirteen years old when he came to live with us.

Christmas that year was so exciting for me. I got the opportunity to see my father who came to Miss Mazy's to be with us on Christmas Eve. I can remember sneaking into the living room where I was able to see my father and mother placing the gifts for us under the Christmas tree. That's when I discovered that Santa Claus wasn't the old man with a white beard and a big stomach dressed in a red suit. It was really my parents who bought our gifts and placed them under the tree. There were other times when my mother would have to separate my siblings and I in other homes for Christmas in order for us to receive gifts, because she couldn't afford to buy us any. We didn't have much, but the love that our mother demonstrated to us spoke volumes.

After some time my father and mother reconciled with each other, and we moved to an apartment building on West Farms Road. That's when I experienced my father fighting my mother. This event frightened me very much. One evening my father and Aaron fought after Aaron jumped into a physical fight that my father and mother were having. My father almost cut Aarons thumb off of his hand. I stood there in shock, screaming as my brother's hand was bleeding profusely. Now I truly began to understand why my mother had to leave my father.

Some of the happier times in my life would be when my mother picked me up from school. She would take me past the fresh farm markets. They would be selling some of everything. They sold fresh meats, fish, vegetables and fruit. They even sold little yellow chicks. One day I asked my mother if she would buy me some of the chicks, and she did. She bought me twelve little chicks, which I carried home in a small cage. I had no idea how to care for them, and everyday when I came home from school at least one or two of them would be dead. They weren't able to survive in the environment that I had them in. I was deeply saddened that I wasn't able to keep my baby chicks from dying.

After some time had passed, we moved back to our own apartment at 832 Dawson Street. I can recall one evening my parents having an argument, and my father locking the entire family out on the fire escape outside of our living room. I remember being very afraid, and not being able to understand why my father did this. Not long after this incident we had to move to the basement of the same building. During this period of time my father was still very much in our lives. Many of their arguments would involve him physically assaulting her and then having to escape the house before the police arrived. Even though there was a great deal of chaos and confusion in our home, the overwhelming love that I felt from my family was able to give me some semblance of happiness. I was also happy that my father was still with us even though he and my mother didn't get along very well. One morning before going to school, I purposely hid one of my one pair of shoes so that I wouldn't have to go to school. I wanted to stay home with my dad. I remember him making me a bowl of watery cereal with a little bit of Carnation condensed canned milk and a lot of sugar. And although I didn't enjoy it very much, I had to eat every bit of it.

Later that day my father took me to the store, and bought me an Almond Joy candy bar and a Pepsi Cola for himself. I remember that Pepsi Cola was my dad's favorite drink. During the same time frame I can vaguely remember being molested. I can remember being in a bedroom located between the kitchen and the living room. The room didn't have any doors. Either I can't remember or I blocked who touched me out of my mind. Nevertheless I definitely know that even though there was no penetration, someone sexually violated me.

One of the more pleasurable memories I have of my father is when there was snowy weather. My father would get a big pot and pack it with snow. Then he would make us flavored snow cream. It tasted very good. My father was a very meticulous person. My siblings and I each had a part in keeping the house clean. We had to mop the floors and wax them with our hands. Then my brothers, sister and I would find old pieces of rags and use them to dance all over the wooden floors until they shined. We made the best out of the hard work that we had to do. My father worked at a bakery on the night shift, and in the morning he would always bring home the leftover doughnuts that his boss had given him. And in spite of the fact that my father wasn't an educated man, I would learn much from him without him having a lot to say. As I matured into a young woman, I would visit my father in his apartment in Harlem New York on 116th Street. He knew how to cook, and would always prepare his really good fried chicken dinner with buttered white rice and a vegetable for me. On one of my visits, he took me into his bedroom, opened a dresser drawer and showed off his immaculately clean folded underwear. Sometime later I realized that there was a lesson in everything my father showed me. In his own way, my father was preparing me for when I would be married.

Not long after we moved into the basement apartment my father and mother separated for good. The apartment had a few bedrooms, a kitchen, and a bathroom. Outside of the apartment were cement floors, and rooms that looked like horse stables down a dark hallway. There was also a huge furnace in the back of the basement. The doors of the furnace were open and one could see the red hot coals that fueled the fire that kept our apartment heated. Uncle Bernie lived with us also, and I believe that he slept in one of those rooms that was in the basement. My mother had recently bought me a brand new toy doll baby, and somehow it ended up being accidently burned up in the furnace. When Uncle Bernie told me about my doll I cried profusely for days. My mother had just bought me some new clothes for my doll and now it was destroyed.

The apartment where we lived was located not too far from Corona Park. During the summer my friend Karen and I would go to the pool that was in the park. One day while at the pool Karen was teaching me how to swim. I was doing pretty well at the shallow end of the pool, but I was terrified of going into the deeper end. One day while we were at the pool I was able to muster up enough courage to dive into the water. However, I didn't realize that I had dived into the five foot end of the pool until I felt myself sinking down to the bottom of it. Suddenly I couldn't breathe. I was drowning. Fortunately I wasn't down there too long before Karen jumped in and saved my life. After that happened to me, I developed a fear of swimming.

Karen and I knew this elderly lady who we would visit sometime. We would go to her apartment on Fridays to pick up the empty soda bottles that she saved for us. During that period of time soda bottles could be recycled, and we would redeem five cents for each bottle returned. I enjoyed the two of us getting money for the bottles then running to the store to buy bags of candy, popcorn, and sometimes home cooked french fries. However my fondest memories of going to her apartment were when we would go to her house and she would let me play her huge old piano. I would play songs I knew by ear. I believe she loved us visiting her on those Fridays. Karen also had an aunt named Veronica, and we loved to listen to her West Side Story album. We loved singing "Maria" and the Jets songs. We would dance as if we were in the movie. Karen would later tell me that we had been in a talent show. Our mothers worked hard all the time, and so we found ourselves wandering the neighborhood looking to have fun. We never realized that we were two little girls in a dangerous world. I often walked with Karen to her father's house so she could get money from him. One day we ventured off into this dangerous park called Horseshoe Park. We had been told not to go there, because Horseshoe Park was gang territory, but we didn't even know what a gang was. We were just a couple of little girls out having fun. Karen and I and some other girls walked to the park, which was pretty far from the block we lived on. As soon as we got there some Hispanic guys chased me all the way home. I remember running as fast as my little feet could carry me. but I couldn't run fast enough. I was almost caught by one of the gang members, but a little old lady (who I later referred to as my angel) stepped between me and the guy, and that afforded me the opportunity to escape him and run all the way home. Karen said that she came back to get me several times, but she couldn't find me. I was never so happy to see Dawson Street. I never set foot in Horseshoe Park again.

Every summer the Sixty Center sponsored an annual bus ride to Jones Beach. I thoroughly enjoyed this outing. As we rode the bus I always knew when we were close to arriving, because I could always smell the beach's salty sea water. When we arrived the staff would escort us into a large room that was equipped with bathroom stalls and showers where we would change into our swimwear. This same room allowed us to also participate in arts and crafts and play a variety of games. When we went to the actual beach, I wouldn't go into the water. Instead, I would stand at the edge of the water on the sand, and dip my feet into the water. Standing at the water's edge always gave me a feeling of being pulled into the sea. I really loved that feeling. Afterward, we would all meet back at the room to eat lunch. We were given a sandwich, a drink, and one fruit. We would finish our crafts and take them home.

One day my mother was involved in an incident where she accidentally took an overdose of pills. I distinctly remember being very frightened as my family members were repeatedly banging on the bathroom door in an attempt to get her to come out. When she finally emerged, she was immediately taken to the hospital. My mother had been through a lot of turmoil with my father. and she was raising six children by herself. After coming back from the hospital my mother never spoke of this incident, so I never knew if she planned to take her own life. All I knew as a little girl was that I was often afraid. Sometime later my mother starting dating a man named Mr. Eddie. Mr. Eddie was a chauffeur for a white family, and he would often take us for rides to New Jersey in their limousine. Unfortunately (or fortunately, as the case may be) my mother's relationship didn't last very long. My sister and I both heard from a close friend that Mr. Eddie wanted my mother, but didn't want the six children that came with her. It wasn't long after she discovered the true intent of his heart that she ended it with him. My mother was a spiritually and naturally beautiful woman who probably could have had any man at that time. However, she wasn't going to allow any men into her life that wouldn't accept her children.

Not too long after her breakup with Mr. Eddie my mother would meet and fall in love with the man whom I would eventually receive as my Pops. His name was Willie Otha Jones, but he was fondly referred to as "Bokay." Bokay had just been honorably discharged from the Army. He was a veteran of the Korean War. At our first meeting, Bokay had on his green military uniform. He was a handsome young man. My mother called him "Otha," and he called her "Peach." As soon as I saw him, I liked him immediately. I would talk to him a mile a minute. One day he sang this song to me. "You talk too much, you worry me to death..." He had a unique way of making me laugh.

My mother and Bokay started dating, and I could tell that there was something special between them. One day Mom sat us all down, and asked us what we thought about her getting married to Bokay. Well, I couldn't speak for my siblings, but I was super excited about the idea. I knew even back then, that in addition to wanting my mother, I also needed a father in my life.

I loved all of my brothers and sister very much. My brother Vernon worked on a delivery truck that delivered fresh milk to the surrounding neighborhoods. The milk bottles were stored in these gray metal crates. Vernon always made sure that he brought us fresh milk. My eldest brother Aaron was nicknamed "Lil Bro." He met and fell in love with a young lady named Johnella. She lived in the Tilden Projects located in the North Bronx. My next to the youngest brother was named David. He was a tough guy and could defend himself well when he had to fight. As a result his friends nicknamed him "Dukin'." My youngest brother Ronnie had a lot of Puerto Rican friends. He loved hanging out with them and eating Puerto Rican foods. My big sister Joyce was a very quiet person back then, but she was my protector. She would protect me even if it meant that she had to physically fight for me. Joyce was truly a big sister.

Not too long after Bokay came into our lives, my mother started attending a small storefront holiness church. It was across the street from where we lived. Pastor Tucker and his wife were very lovely people. I loved going to church. I remember my mother bouncing me up and down on her lap as she sang along with the music. My mother also participated in teaching YPAC (Young People Association Class). We learned chapters, and verses from the Bible. We also performed Christmas plays and for Easter, we recited poetry. I am certain that back then my mother was a convert to Christianity.

When I was ten years old, my mother's new husband moved us to a house that his sister and brother-in-law owned in Brooklyn. I would later refer to them as my Uncle Vick and Aunt Marie. The house was a beautiful two story brownstone with a finished basement, and was located at 2178 Strauss Street. Uncle Vick and Aunt Marie had two daughters. The oldest was named Velma and was seven. Her younger sister was named Voncile, and was five. It was very hard for me to move away from the Bronx. After all, my best friend Karen lived there. But I had to admit, we had moved to a much better environment than the neighborhood in the Bronx. My family and I lived in the downstairs apartment, while my uncle and aunt, the Cunninghams lived upstairs. Joyce and I still shared a room, but it was much larger than the last one. My brothers shared a large bedroom together, and my parents their own room. It was the biggest and nicest place we had lived in since originally moving to New York.

My Relationship with my new cousins got off to a great start. I would go upstairs to their apartment everyday and play with them. We would have tea parties, and play with their dolls. Sometimes I would stay with them overnight on weekends. During that time, or maybe even before then I had developed a bed wetting problem that lasted well into my teen years. And although my mother attributed it to my being nervous, years later I would learn that it was actually a physical problem.

Uncle Vick and Aunt Marie were secular people, and on the weekends they would socialize with their friends. They played cards and drank beer. Uncle Vick would always buy us the large sized bag of Wise Potato Chips. We would eat the chips together in the girls bedroom. But when Uncle Vick and Aunt Marie went out we really had fun. This is when we would dress up in my aunt's clothes and put on her heels, and become the Supremes. We would sing their song "Stop! In The Name of Love." I was Diana Ross, Velma was Mary Wilson, and Voncile was Florence Henderson. We were very good, and it was very exciting imitating them.

After getting married to Pops, my mother stopped going to church, and started going to beautician school to study beauty culture in order to become a licensed beautician. My mother also enlisted my assistance. She brought her manicure case with all of its equipment home with her so that she could teach me how to do manicures. My mother loved doing hair. One day before getting her license, she gave Ronnie a haircut, and left little bald patches on his head. I really believe that she used his head as a practice exercise before taking her class. Sometimes my mother and Pops would socialize with my aunt and uncle in their basement. One day I went downstairs to the basement, and to my surprise I saw my mother drinking a beer. I had never seen her drunk, or drink anything alcoholic before. My mom was a plain woman who taught us the values of love and family. And she always prayed with and for us.

We stayed at 2178 Strauss Street for two years before moving to the East New York section of Brooklyn. After a while, I lost count of exactly how many times we moved. My parents moved us into an upstairs apartment of a two story brownstone house at 151 Legion Street. I believe the reason my parents moved away from Uncle Vick and Aunt Marie was based on a disagreement they had between them. It wasn't long after that move that my mother and Pops began fighting.

Joyce and I stayed in the bedroom adjacent to my parents bedroom, and we would hear them arguing. My brother Vernon would interfere, and physically fight Pops. Of course it was his way of protecting our mother. By this time my eldest brother Aaron was married, and had two sons of his own. On this occasion Vernon and Pops were fighting outside on the balcony of my room. I saw Vernon almost fall from the balcony. All of the arguing and fighting caused me to be extremely nervous and I had no idea of what all the fighting was about. Later I learned that it wasn't our place to interfere in their arguments. However, none of us were just going to stand there and allow our mother to be physically abused.

Joyce and I shared a bedroom that was adjacent to my parents room, and it was in that room that I started being sexualy molested by a family member. He would sneak into my room late at night and pull my panties down and fondle my private parts. Because I was so very young, and it felt good I never said anything to anyone about what this family member was doing to me. Somehow I was consciously aware that what was happening to me was wrong. However, I failed to listen to my conscience, and as a result growing up in a dysfunctional family I eventually became introverted. As a result I began to cultivate an imaginary place in my mind that I would escape to so that I wouldn't have to face a reality that was much too hard for me to deal with. I'm not certain how long this family member was violating me, but I do know that what he did to me left an indelible scar in my subconscious. I never told Joyce, who was my closest friend at that time, what happened to me. It was during this period of my life when I became the little girl, hiding in the corner of my mind. I would eventually have very conflicting feelings about this family member, because this same person who played bass guitar, and played it well, tried to teach me how to play. To my mind he could have been trying to cozy up to me in an attempt to encourage me not to expose him. Some time after I learned that he had a problem that he would never face up to. Eventually I was able to forgive him for the part that he played in destroying my innocence. However, this childhood violation would become an integral part of my sexual misconduct in the years that followed.

At the age of twelve I was singing in the school chorus at Somers Junior High School. Mrs. Shane was our music teacher. We performed in shows such as "Porgy and Bess," and "The Sound of Music." I discovered that singing allowed me to escape the dysfunctionality of my world, and gave me a sense of peace within myself. I sang in the alto section of the choir. I really loved chorus rehearsals and I really got a charge out of dress rehearsals the day before the show was to be performed. I would get nervous on opening night. The crowded audience would get me excited. Mrs Shane's face would beam with a huge bright smile as she directed us. There was a tough guy in the chorus named China. China was a great singer, and when he belted out his song, "It Ain't Necessarily So" you could see that he was just a young man with a beautiful voice. All our voices would blend together to make this wonderful sound. It was very invigorating. The different colored-foot lights at the foot of the stage would be shining out into the audience. It made me feel like we were on Broadway.

While attending Somers Junior High School, I met a girl named Elsie with whom I developed a friendship. Elsie and her family were from Panama, and she was the only girl among a few older brothers. Elsie's mother worked hard and had taught her how to cook. She knew how to prepare this corned beef and rice dish that she would allow me to sample. Elsie would also visit with me some of the time. She and I were in the ninth grade when we went to our first discotheque. Ironically it was called "Satan's Pit." And, although I was shy, dancing became my outlet.

Lunchtime was a very special treat at Somers JHS. There was an elderly woman who sold knishes from her rolling cart everyday. She charged thirty five cents a knish. They were the best homemade knishes that I ever tasted. In school my grades were pretty average. If I had the help that I needed I'm sure that I could have done much better. However, everyone was living their own lives and they didn't have a lot of time for me. My eldest brother Aaron recently told me that he remembers me always having my head in a book, and that he thought I was very smart. I wanted to be a teenager very much, and when I turned thirteen my mother bought me a bazooka corsage. It had thirteen bubblegums on it. I thought; Now I'm a young adult. How far from the truth that was! I soon learned that I wasn't mature enough to make any correct decisions on my own. But at thirteen I felt that I was ready for the world. But was the world ready for me?

We had a whole lot of fun on Legion Street. I didn't have many friends on the block, but my sister and I would stay out late. One day we met the "Carter" family (no relation). They lived at the end of Legion Street. Their father was a pastor, and their mother, a nurse. They had a sister who was my age. Her name was Denise, and we would hang out together sometime. One day I was in the park that was across the street from where we lived, and I met the "Williams" sisters. They could really sing well.

They also were from the south, and had moved to our block. One time I sang with them, and on another occasion we were walking together on Pitkin Avenue, which was just a few blocks from where I lived. It was on a Sunday afternoon, and as we were walking, we passed by this small storefront Holiness church. We could hear the congregation singing, and hear music playing. I could hear the drums beating, the organ playing, and the unique sound of a Hawaiian guitar. It sounded like they were having a good time. We peeked inside the church and decided to go in. Well, to our surprise, they called us up to the front to sing. Afterward, I ran home to let my mother know about this fire-baptized church called "St. James Holiness Church." One Sunday, my mother went to visit the church.

My mother would always have Bible studies with us. It was a traditional habit of hers. One evening, after sitting us down for the study, my brother Vernon started asking her questions about the Gospel. Ultimately he went to St. James Holiness, repented, and received the LORD Jesus Christ as His LORD and Savior. St. James Holiness Church would have what is known as "Tarrying Services" every Thursday evening. These services were designed to help new converts to receive the "baptism of the Holy Ghost." The older women of the congregation, who were dressed in all white garments, would lead the new converts to the altar and pray with them. They would instruct the converts to repeatedly call the name of Jesus in a very rapid fashion. This exercise would result in the convert talking so fast that they would begin speaking in another language, or what the Bible referred to as "unknown tongues." Prior to his salvation experience, Vernon was always getting into trouble. So, as you can well imagine, he shocked and surprised everyone by the radical changes that he exhibited in his life after his salvation experience. During this period of time, our eldest brother Aaron was married and living in Manhattan, and as soon as he heard that Vernon had given his life to the LORD, he came to Brooklyn to see if what he'd heard was true.

Every Thursday I would attend the tarrying service held at St. James Holiness. It seemed so hard for the new converts to receive the Holy Spirit. I disliked what happened to them as they repeated the name of Jesus so fast that they would be frothing at the mouth. It really looked disgusting. The ladies in the white dresses would be right there wiping the spittle from their mouths, and discarding the tissues in a basket. It was during one of these services that my sister Joyce gave her life to the LORD. However, by the time she was sixteen she had already backslid.

One evening, while everyone had gone to church, I was home alone, and my sister's friend Deborah came over with a young man that I was crushing on. Not realizing what I was doing at the time, I allowed Deborah to influence me to let the young man into my bedroom, as she talked me into giving up my virginity to him. After Deborah left the house, I engaged in sexual intercourse with him. It was really painful when he penetrated me. Yes, it's true. I had a terrible crush on him, but I should have never allowed him to take away what should have been so precious to me. Once again my innocence had been violated, but this time it was with my consent. Not only did I experience physical pain, but I also felt so ashamed of myself. I had given up something precious of myself that should have been held in reserve for the man that I would eventually marry. I really had no idea of the consequences that I had incurred upon myself, because of this sinful act. I was still a child, sucking my finger, and wetting my bed. Unfortunately no one in the family had taken the time to teach me about how important it was that I remain a virgin until I was married. Something terrible happened to me after that. I began allowing that same young man to take me into back alleys on our block to have sex with him. I discovered that I had been thrust into an adult experience that I wasn't prepared for at all. Where were the adults in my life? No fourteen year old child should be allowed to go through what I went through. During this same time, I also began menstruating. I learned a little about menstruating in school, and from same experienced teenagers who talked in general about it. The first time that I began bleeding was on a Sunday morning, and although I couldn't wait to have this experience, I feared not having anyone around to explain it to me. My brother Aaron's wife, Johnella, tried to explain to me what I should do in order to take care of myself. When my mother came home from church, I told her about having my period. I don't remember her ever talking to me about having my period, and what having that experience would mean for me. After I talked to her, she bought some sanitary napkins for me.

My mother worked at a beauty parlor on Fulton Street in Brooklyn. She took me to the beauty parlor with her every Saturday. Sometime before we left to go home, she would do my hair. I really loved being with my mom. I always enjoyed watching the ladies getting their hair done. My mother would send me to a local restaurant to buy her and the ladles that worked with her their lunch. I had an aunt named Doll who later opened a restaurant along with her then boyfriend, right next door to the beauty parlor. So, after Aunt Doll opened her restaurant, I would purchase everyone's lunch from her.

During that time I still went to Strauss Street to visit with my cousins Velma and Voncile. And sometimes Velma would come to my house and spend the weekend with me. My eldest brother, Aaron was the director of the youth choir at St. James Holiness Church. Both Velma and I sang in the choir. Sometimes Aaron would take the entire choir in a van to the neighborhood White Castle's Hamburgers restaurant. I loved eating the little cheeseburgers with onion rings and milk shakes. Our church sponsored bus outings for us. We would go to the amusement park at Bear Mountain. Velma and I sang a song called "I'll Trade a Lifetime for Just One Day in Paradise." I also sang a solo called. "It Pays to serve Jesus." However, it wasn't until years later that I would realize the true significance of that song.

After graduating from Somers JHS at the age of fourteen, we moved to a better section of Brooklyn called Crown Heights. I started going to Clara Barton VHS, and I was also still seeing the young man who had taken my virginity. We weren't boyfriend and girlfriend, but I continued having sex with him. However, I could never enjoy it, because it was so painful. By the time I had reached fifteen years old, I still hadn't gone out on an official date. I was shy, and because of that, I decided to go to an all girls high school. I started Clara Barton VHS in the tenth grade. And although I kept up my grades, I had an average GPA. My desire had been to become a registered nurse since I was ten years old, and now my opportunity to fulfill my dream had finally come. However, by the time I reached the eleventh grade, my GPA still didn't allow me to enter the licensed practical nursing program. I landed in the nursing assistant program. While in the eleventh grade I met a young lady who became a distraction to me. I also met a friend of my brother Ronnie named Norman. Norman lived next door to us on Sterling Place. Norman and I started officially dating, and he became my first boyfriend. As a teenager I naturally wanted lo fit in with the kids on the block. I understood popularity as hanging out with who I perceived to be the popular crowd. At that time I hadn't realized that this crowd wasn't really popular. They were just the people that the enemy had assigned to my life as a distraction in order to deter me from the plans that God had for my life. At the age of sixteen I started smoking and drinking beer.

My relationship with Norman seemed like a one sided affair. He could come over to my house, but I was never invited over to his house. As far as I could see, his parents just knew me as the girl next door. Norman and I began having sex immediately. The roof of my house was attached to the sun porch in the back of his house. All I had to do was sneak into his bedroom from my window whenever he would knock on his bedroom wall. How foolish of me to think that Norman loved or even cared about me. I had become a promiscuous young girl who was a victim of low self-esteem. I thought I was in love with him, but I really didn't know anything about love, because of my own immaturity.

I was still attending St. James Holiness Church in Brownsville Brooklyn along with my family every Sunday. My older brother Vernon didn't allow us to stay home from church like the other kids on the block. It was mandatory that we be in church every Sunday. Every summer all of the kids on the block would come and hang out on our stoop until around midnight. But we could never hang out on theirs. Pops hated this and would angrily run everyone off of our stoop as soon as he came home. He never liked to see all of us teenagers hanging out in front of his home. My younger brother Ronnie always had company over to our house all the time. As a consequence, our home became the neighborhood hangout. I just knew that I was having the time of my life. By the time Ronnie and I hit eighteen we vowed that we weren't going to church anymore. For some reason to us eighteen seemed to be the age of our maturity, but I wasn't mature. We had a good friend named Kevin. He lived a few houses down the block from us. He and I were very good friends. One summer he became seriously ill to the point of not being able to walk. His respiratory system had shut down and he had to be hospitalized. He was taken to a hospital in Manhattan. Most of the kids on the block went to see him. When I went to see him I was shocked to see that the doctors had done a tracheostomy procedure on his throat that left him unable to speak. Kevin also had to go through extensive rehabilitation in order to learn how to walk again. He had suffered from some type of neuromuscular disease. After numerous visits that summer, Kevin was finally able to walk and talk a little. My brother and his girlfriend, and Norman and I, and a few of his other friends would sneak reefer to him so that he could get high. We were so crazy back then. Nothing seemed to phase us at all. After a lengthy stay in the hospital, Kevin was eventually discharged. On one of our crazy weekends, my cousin Velma had a party at her house in Brownsville. We took Kevin with us to her party. We were a wild and crazy bunch who loved having fun. Kevin and I would sing Carol King's song "It's Too late." He also loved to hear me sing Stevie Wonder's song Love's In Need of Love Today."

Meantime at 698 Sterling Place, my brother David had been drafted into the Army, and was deployed to Vietnam. It was the year 1968. I wrote him letters every week. One Christmas our family sent him a care package full of goodies. And after we hadn't heard from him in several weeks, my mother was very afraid. However she continued to pray and believe in God for his safe return. I don't think anyone realized that I was very afraid of losing my brother to the war. There were songs out about the Vietnam War, and I would always sing them when I thought about David. After about a month, we finally heard from him. David finally came home from the war. The Army officials had written to my mother informing her that David would probably be suffering from Shellshock, known years later as PTSD. They told her that he would be emotionally scarred, and that he would also have physical scars from exposure to Agent Orange. When David came home we were so happy to see him. However, David would later be the one who introduced my friends and I to marijuana.

One of the major blunders that I committed in high school was when I was in the eleventh grade. During that period of my life I spent a lot of time goofing off instead of focusing on my classes. In the summer of 1969 I trained for eight weeks at Kings County Hospital in their nursing assistant program. At the end of the summer, I completed the course with high scores, I now had the potential to become a registered nurse. Unfortunately, I was hanging out with someone who I allowed to negatively influence me. She trained in the same program that I did, but worked on a different unit. During my senior year of high school, I trained in the hospital's Cooperative Program. This program allowed me to acquire practical experience by working for two weeks, and then I would return to school for two weeks. I also had the additional advantage of being able to develop my ability to work with the patients (which I loved doing) and in addition to that, bring home a paycheck. At that time the hospitals had what they called unit wards. Units were composed of at least ten to fifteen patients per unit. I was assigned to do total care for at least five patients. This included giving them complete baths, taking their temperatures, and making their beds. I had an excellent supervisor who advised me to stay in the program and apply for their registered nursing course of study. However, the state of mind that I was in at the time wouldn't allow me to. So, I declined. It was the worst choice that I have ever made In my life, and to this day I regret it. In my last year of high school our senior class went on a boat ride to Bear Mountain. Both myself and a friend of mine decided to hide some rum in our pocketbooks for the trip. I drank so much of it until I became sick.

After graduating in 1970, I decided not to go back to Kings County Hospital to work. I looked for a job in the Wall Street area of New York. I wanted to trade emptying bedpans for working in an office. It took persistence, but I finally landed a job on Williams Street in a company as a file clerk. I really felt quite dignified working in the famous Wall Street financial district of New York. I would get up early in the morning, wash and dress myself. And then, I would leave my house, and walk to the Franklin Avenue train station, and take the train into downtown Manhattan. I would read my newspaper while riding the train. I guess that made me feel rather important. I mean, after all, what did I know? I was only eighteen years old, and here I was, working with the big shots! I had a German supervisor who was very strict, but if one got their work done she would demonstrate the better side of her personality to them. I met this young lady from down south. Her name was Edna, and we became good buddies, eating our lunch together. Unfortunately for me, although I didn't have any reason to, I picked up the very bad habit of pilfering things that didn't belong to me. I didn't make a lot of money, but for an eighteen year old, I was making enough money. I didn't have to steal from anyone. My problem was getting away with it made me feel as though I would never get caught. After all, it was so easy. However, I was truly operating in a delusion of my own making. My friend Edna told me that she thought I was crazy. I would take her with me to the clothing boutiques around our job. While there, I would take three outfits into the dressing room but I would hide one outfit under two of the others. This way the dressing room attendant would see me carrying two outfits instead of three. Once I was in the dressing room, I would put the outfit that I intended to steal in my very large pocketbook. Ironically we think we're getting away when God sees everything we do. I stole because I thought it was fun to be able to get away with it. But at nineteen I was incarcerated for stealing and spent twelve hours in a Manhattan jail.

I enrolled in New York Community College in the winter of 1971. My step-father's GI benefits allowed me to take their nursing courses free of charge. Unfortunately I allowed an old friend of mine to negatively influence me. And instead of focusing on my goal I started hanging out, partying and getting high. Finally, after one semester, I dropped out. As a result of my inappropriate behavior, I ended up disappointing my parents. I especially disappointed my Pops who really wanted me to go to Duke University in North Carolina. In retrospect, if I hadn't allowed myself to be distracted, I would have been the first college graduate in my family. Instead I destroyed my dream of becoming an RN by getting high, partying and being promiscuous. After dropping out of college. I took a job with a temporary nursing agency. The name of the agency is Medical Personnel Pool. During the week I would do live-in assignments, and on the weekends I would return home.

My first assignment with the Medical Personnel Pool agency was in a nice quiet neighborhood in Queens. It would take an hour to get to work.

I was assigned to work with an elderly caucascian woman who was bedridden. She had a son whose name was Hugh Jones. Mr. Jones had been born in London, England and he worked as an accountant in the financial district of Manhattan. Most of the time my work day was very boring. After caring for Mrs. Jones, I really didn't have much to do for the rest of the day. I would bathe her every morning, feed her breakfast and lunch, and administer her medication. When Mr. Jones came home from work, he would prepare dinner for us. I was given a small bedroom that was upstairs. This room was very clean and neat. It had a bed, and a desk with a lamp on it, a dresser drawer, and a closet for my clothes.

At that time Mr. Jones was a single man in his late forties. He also introduced me to his sister and her family who were Christians. Although he was very attentive to his mother, I soon observed that he drank excessively, especially on the weekends. He told me that he made the choice to be the caretaker in his family. I believe that was one reason why he never married. One Friday evening after dinner, Mr. Jones had been drinking for quite some time, and to my extreme shock, surprise, and amazement, he tried to kiss me. I immediately turned my face away from him. He was much older than me, and I certainly wasn't going to take advantage of his feeling(?) by pretending that I cared for him in that way. After all, this very sweet man was a WWII veteran who had fought in the battle at Normandy in 1944. Mr Jones had often also talked to me at length about his experiences in the war. Seeing so many people die, (many of them his friends), had taken a tremendous toll on his psycho-emotional state.

After a few months working with Mrs. Jones, she died, and my assignment ended. However. Mr. Jones and I kept in touch with each other. He would always encourage me to go back to school and get my degree to become a registered nurse. In fact, he always told me that I was born to be a nurse. He even offered to pay my tuition and asked my mother for her permission to do so. Mr. Jones wrote me a check for two thousand dollars. And once again, I made the wrong choice. Instead of going bock to school, I spent the money, and forfeited my opportunity to go back to school and get my nursing degree. And yet although I deeply disappointed him, Mr Jones never gave up on me. Although I didn't realize it at the time, the providential protection and core of the LORD was operating in my life. I now understand that Mr. Hugh Jones was serving me in the capacity of a guardian angel.

One day Mr. Jones asked me if I would marry him. I immediately said no, because I knew that I didn't love him like that. However, I did love him for the fact that I knew that he genuinely cared about me. In time I would understand that in all actuality by taking his money and not using it for his intended purpose I had taken advantage of his goodness to me. And, for that, I am heartily sorry. I didn't understand it at the time, but Mr. Jones had really been like a father to me.

That same year in 1971 I went on a bus outing with some of my friends. While riding the bus I began to feel sick. My boyfriend

Norman sat next to me. I told him that I felt sick to my stomach, and he quickly asked me if I thought that I might be pregnant. Wow!!! To my surprise, the thought that I might get pregnant had never entered my mind!!! During that period of time, I wasn't even paying enough attention to know whether I missed having my period or not. Suddenly I began to realize that something was terribly wrong. Everything that I had eaten while on the outing that day I vomited. Later on, after going home, I spoke to a family friend and she told me about a doctor that I could see in order to get help. That week I went to see the doctor. His office was located in a brownstone basement apartment not too far from where I lived. After he examined me, the doctor confirmed that I was indeed several months pregnant. I was completely surprised and demanded proof of his findings. He instructed me to feel my stomach, and as I did, I could feel the swell of my lower abdomen. I was pregnant with no knowledge of ever having missed my period. Suddenly it dawned on me that I had been so busy hanging out, getting high, and having fun that I missed the extraordinary reality that I was carrying a living human being in my own body!!!

As soon as I made my boyfriend aware that I was pregnant, his instant reaction was that I should immediately have an abortion. At that moment the first person I thought about was my sister. She was having her second child out of wedlock, and I didn't want to disappoint my parents with another illegitimate pregnancy. I frantically began to think about what I should do. But I realized that I didn't have that much time to think about it, because the baby was still growing inside of me. I panicked and scheduled an appointment with Planned Parenthood in order to have the abortion. Unfortunately, in my panicked state of mind, the most important reality that I never considered was that by aborting my baby, I would be committing murder. It is true that under Roe vs Wade I had a legal right to have an abortion, but what the law and my Planned Parenthood counselor didn't inform me of was the horrific psycho-emotional consequences that I would suffer by committing such a heinous crime against God. The Law of God declares "Thou shall not kill." This is one of the Ten Commandments that I learned in Bible study. As a consequence of having aborted my baby, I became imprisoned by this deep dark secret in the corner of my mind where the little girl in me resided.

The first time I went to the clinic I was given a pregnancy test, and referred to an abortion counselor. The counselor spoke with me and gave me an appointment to return. When I returned, I was taken into a room and injected with a salt-based solution. After which, I was sent back home and told to wait until I went into labor. That night while in my bedroom I began to experience an excruciating level of pain. It was unlike any other night that I had ever experienced. I'll never forget how hard it rained and how acutely alone I felt. I remember tapping on the wall adjacent to Norman's house in order to ask him if he would take me to Kings County Hospital. He consented and when we arrived at the hospital Norman walked away, leaving me all alone to bear the full weight of murdering our child. I was cramping terribly as I lay in my hospital bed wishing that my mom was with me. My mom would never have allowed me to do such a terrible thing, but it was too late. My baby was actively being murdered right there in my womb, and I was the one doing it. Although I was too afraid to let my mother know about my pregnancy, deep in my heart I knew that she would have accepted it, and never allowed me to abort her grandchild. I would have never had an abortion. I felt so cold when the nursing assistant came into my room, She seemed icily indifferent, and she had an angry expression on her face. After all, God had given me a precious gift and I was killing it. The moment had come for me to expel my dead baby. As I went into the bathroom across the hall from me, and was given a cold steel bedpan. I distinctly remember seeing this bloody blob emerging from my womb and falling into the bedpan. I looked at it in amazement and asked "What was that?" She looked at me and very unceremoniously said "That's the baby."

After going through such an horrendous ordeal, it seemed as if it only took a minute for the hospital to discharge me. Norman didn't come to get me. Neither did anyone else for that matter. I had to catch a cab, and go home without him. When I got there, I was still experiencing intense abdominal cramping and I remember having an overwhelming feeling of abandonment. I had to experience going through this night without any support. I really thought that Norman loved me, but the cruel reality that I had to face was that he had left me to go through the murder of our child without him.

After I had the abortion, my life began spiraling downward. As I tried to bury the horrible act that I committed, I started drinking excessively. I blacked out on more than one occasion, and while trying desperately to get someone to pay attention to me, I became promiscuous. However, in the midst of all that was happening and had happened to me, I was somehow able to continue working for the nursing agency and hanging out as though nothing had happened, but deep in the nether regions of my soul I was hurting, because I had chosen to destroy the precious life that the LORD had given me.

One of the high points in my life at that time was the birth of my niece. I was with my sister Joyce on August 18, 1971 when she gave birth to her second child, Chauntele Staci.

I remember the birth of Chauntele, our first girl grandchild and how much joy and excitement she brought into our home. The next day I remember being so excited that my girlfriends and I went to Macy's department store in Manhattan on a shoplifting spree. We were able to leave the store successfully. But, by the time we got to the train station the police were waiting for us, and we were taken back to Macy's and questioned. Ironically my friends were released, and got away scott free but they arrested and handcuffed me. I couldn't believe that I got caught! To my utter and complete surprise, I was totally unaware that we were being surveilled by the store detectives the entire time that we were shoplifting. Because I was very small at that time, somehow I managed to slip my hands out of the handcuffs and escape. I ran away from them as fast as I could, but lo no avail, I was caught again and put into a police van. There were no windows in the van, so I couldn't see where they were taking me. Upon arriving I discovered that I had been taken to the city jail in Manhattan.

I remember being allowed one phone call, which I used to call my sister Joyce. I could always count on her to get me out of trouble. I was so ashamed and embarrassed about being arrested for stealing that I begged Joyce not to say anything to our mother about it. Once I was fingerprinted, I was placed in a cell with a lot of prostitutes. A few hours later an officer came and transferred me to a different cell in which was a young lady who had been arrested for forging checks. Earlier that day I'd bought my sister a sandwich from Blimpies intending to give it to her when I visited her at the hospital. Little did I know that I would end up spending twelve hours of that day in the lockup. By the time I was brought into the courtroom Joyce had already sent her boyfriend Raymond and my brother David to meet me there. When I walked out into the courtroom I had no idea of the severity of the crime that I had committed. Trembling and afraid, I humbly stood before the judge as the guilt and shame of what I'd done overwhelmed me. I was given a date to return to court. When Joyce came home from the hospital with Chauntele, she accompanied me to my court date where I was sentenced to pay a fine of $100.00. After going through that horrible experience I learned my lesson and never had any more trouble with the law.

I remember being so happy when my sister Joyce returned home from the hospital with her baby girl. I was the one who helped Joyce to take care of her. We made up a cradle bed in our small bedroom for Chauntele to stay in. Everyone in the family loved baby Chauntele, and aggressively competed to babysit with her every weekend. Because Chauntele was so close to my heart, whenever her mother went away. I was the one who took care of. I took great joy in feeding, bathing, and just seeing to her overall care. And although Joyce was very young at the time of her first child's birth, I remember being just as happy. I was on the playground during lunchtime at Somers Junior High when Darryl was born. At the announcement of Darryl's birth my heart leaped for joy, and I could hardly wait to get home to see him.

Darryl was nine months old when Joyce returned to school. One day while we were at school, my mother, (who was a professional beautician), decided that Darryl needed a haircut. Darryl had a beautiful head of curly hair. Our mother cut it all off. When Joyce saw what Mom had done to her son's head, she was furious. But there was nothing that she could say. After all, she was a teenage mother living at home with her parents.

As time progressed, I was given a live-in assignment with an elderly woman who lived in a better section of Brooklyn. I would work with her five days a week. We got along just fine although she didn't trust me at all. Every Friday evening I would order a fifth of Harvey's Bristol Cream sherry for myself, and have it delivered to my patient's apartment. On some occasions I would also allow my boyfriend to come over. One evening, after I had drank my cherry until I was drunk, I fell asleep. My patient awakened to the smell of smoke and began screaming, waking me up. To my own astonishment I had fallen asleep and left the oven on, almost setting the apartment on fire! When she informed her daughter-in-law that I'd nearly burned down her apartment, I vehemently denied it. As a consequence, although I continued working with the agency, they instructed me not to go back to that assignment. Every Saturday morning upon the arrival of my relief, I would leave and begin my weekend off. I would take a cab home, and tip the driver generously. I loved to shop on the weekends. I would go to Greenwich Village in Manhattan, because I didn't want anyone around the way to wear the same outfits that I wore. I wanted to dress and look different than my peers. I would also do a lot of shopping at different boutiques in Brooklyn on Franklin Avenue. I went clubbing on Saturday nights and some Sunday nights. Then on Monday I would have to return to the reality of going back to work.

I was living with my sister when I got pregnant again. Joyce and another friend of mine besought me intensely not to get another abortion, but I wouldn't listen. At first I thought the baby might have been fathered by a guy that I had been currently seeing at the time. However, after doing the calculations, I concluded that the father was indeed my next-door neighbor Norman, the same guy that impregnated me the first time. And it just seemed to be easier this time. After all, I'd already made it known to Norman that I was pregnant again, and he told me that he didn't want me to have the baby. So, I stole my sister's Medicaid card and went to the clinic and murdered my second child. I believe that my heart had been calloused this time, because I didn't feel any remorse. However, after this second abortion I began drinking and smoking marajuana everyday. I wasn't working, and I was constantly drifting in and out of relationships. I began spending a great deal of my time in my bedroom listening to music and sleeping. Drinking, and smoking marajuana, and listening to music allowed me the ability to escape all of my problems. I would play Stevie Wonder's music and sing his songs. 'Mary wants to be a superwoman, but is that really in her head?'

I got pregnant for my third and final time at the age of twenty. This time I determined that I wasn't going to abort this child. However, this pregnancy was an ectopic one. I remember lying down on my mother's living room couch when I suddenly began to experience excruciating pelvic pain. Fortunately, my brother David was there. He called a cab, and when it arrived he lifted me up and carried me out to it. Both he and my mother went with me to Brooklyn Jewish Hospital where The OBGYN doctor informed me that I would have to undergo an emergency surgery to remove one of my fallopian tubes. It wasn't until quite a number of years later that I learned how much of a botched-up job he'd done performing the surgery. This time my entire family was right there with me, including my biological father, Aaron Hall Sr. My dad visited with me everyday. Norman felt so bad for me that he fell into a state of depression also.

Three days after being discharged from the hospital, I discovered that I had lost my live-in job with my elderly patient who lived in Brooklyn. Fortunately I was able to continue getting assignments. I began feeling hopeless, and feeling like my life didn't have any real meaning. Doing drugs and just sleeping had become a great part of my life. Norman wasn't the man that I thought he was, because he started seeing someone else. And after getting high at home, and listening to music that caused me to feel sorry for myself, I started going clubbing by myself. On one occasion I went to the club and saw Norman with his new girlfriend. I became angry and walked right up to her and threatened her. There were incidents when I would call her at her house and tell her "You better leave him alone." I was never a fighter, but drinking often brought out the worst in me. After a while I began feeling suicidal, but I knew that killing myself would be wrong. I had been raised in the house of God, and I knew what his Word said about taking your own life. I knew this guy on the block who I would purchase marijuana from. I would go over to his house and hang out, smoking reefer and drinking alcohol all day. I also experimented with prescription drugs. And one day I went against my own conscience and did some acid. I thank my God that I never had a bad trip. Getting high everyday began taking a heavy toll on my life. Most of the time I felt like I was drifting. The few friends that I did have, I'd lost, or I'd just stopped hanging out with them.

By the time I was twenty one years old my brother Aaron helped me to get a part-time job working on Wall Street. I was hired by an investment firm called Samuel Greenberg and Associates. Although the firm didn't pay me very much money, doing the job actually gave me a great learning experience.

One of the firm's accountants named Lou taught me to do book-keeping for the firm. I was given the responsibility of typing monthly portfolios for each of their clients. And my boss also gave me the assignment of tabulating stocks at the Wall Street trading center. I was afforded the huge opportunity of becoming a great administrative secretary, but I was distracted by my own lifestyle. For example, during my lunch breaks I would foolishly hang out with this young man that I thought had the best reefer I ever smoked. Of course he always thought that I should give him something in return, but I never gave him anything. My lifestyle choices of drugs, drinking, and sex were destroying me. There was an elderly man who worked for the firm. This man supervised the print shop, and had a reputation for sexually harassing the young women on the job. Aaron warned me about him, and also made sure to warn him to leave me alone.

One day while at work, this same man approached me and attempted to sexually harass me. That night after I got home, I mentioned it to my sister. She in turn told Norman about it. The following day while on my way to lunch, I saw Norman approaching me from across the street. He escorted me back upstairs and told me to show him the man who tried to get fresh with me. When I showed him the man, he immediately walked right up to him and gave him a hard slap across his face. I believe that Norman was justified in doing this, because my brother Aaron had previously warned him not to bother his sister in any way.

Around this same time I started hanging out with my younger cousin Bonnie. We hung out with a local band that we would go clubbing with. We would also hang out with the band when they were in rehearsal. It was in one of these rehearsals where I met this Jewish guy named Bruce. Bruce was one of those wild and crazy guys of the seventies that would occasionally hang with Black people. He lived with his parents in Queens, and sometimes would invite me out to his house. But he would only extend this invitation to me when his parents were out of town. Of course this made me feel as though he was ashamed of me. Bruce played the bass guitar really well and wore his hair in a huge curly Afro. Although we dated, our time together was short-lived. One night Bonnie and I went out to a club in Manhattan with Bruce's band. However, before we left I felt like I had to get high. So I unwittingly snorted some heroin that I thought was cocaine, ingested some prescription drugs, and of course I drank some alcohol. That combination of drugs and alcohol should have caused my death, but the LORD had other plans for my life. As soon as we arrived at the club, we sat down at a table with some other young ladies who were also with the band members. It wasn't until later that I found out from Bonnie that I blacked out that night, and couldn't remember anything that happened.

Bonnie recounted to me what had happened that night. She stated that I was so high that I had gotten into an argument with someone. She said that suddenly things had gotten out of control and in the midst of the confusion she lost sight of me. We had come to the club in a van and, not being able to find me, she went to the van and found me there. The next morning when I finally awakened from my drug and alcohol induced stupor, I discovered that I was in Bruce's house in Queens. I was on the floor and I had lost my Afro wig. It was on the floor. And I had a terrible hangover and was suffering from a horrible headache. Ironically, I felt like I had taken an overdose of drugs. It was two weeks before I got over that night, and I never got high like that again.

Not long after that incident my life began to take a turn to what I thought was a better way of life. One day my cousin Bonnie called me. She told me about a cousin that she had (no relation to me) who expressed some interest in getting to know me, and wanted to give me a call. I knew who she was talking about, but I didn't like him very much. I remembered that during our teenage years our family would visit with his family and his extreme disrespect for his parents turned me off. I really surprised myself when I told Bonnie that it was okay for her to give him my phone number. Bonnie informed that he had converted to Islam, At that lime, I didn't know very much about Islam. However, it didn't take long for Rodney to call me. He conveyed that he was very interested in getting to know me, and after talking to him I agreed to meet with him at my house. Upon his arrival we greeted each other and he began telling me about the Nation of Islam and his decision to become a Muslim.

Malcom X was a prominent figure in the Black community, and like everyone else I had heard of him. I knew about his life and tragic death, but I was never really interested in his teachings. After listening and talking to Rodney that evening, I was given a lot of food for thought. He influenced me to consider his reality. After meeting with him on several occasions I was convinced that what he told me was indeed the truth. One evening while Rodney was at my house my old boyfriend Norman who lived next door rang my doorbell. I went to the door and answered it. When I opened the door Norman was standing there and wanted me to let him in. I told him that he couldn't come in, because I had company. I told him that he and I were over. I had given him eight years of my life and now it was time for me to move on. My new Muslim friend seemed to be very serious about Islam and wanted me to go to the Mosque with him. In reality I was very conflicted about this. I realized that converting to Islam and joining the Nation of Islam meant that I must renounce Jesus Christ. How could I convince myself that the One I knew to be the True and Living God all of my life wasn't really God at all. But this Allah was really the true and living God, and that the Honorable Elijah Muhammad was his Prophet? After having sat under the teachings of the Nation of Islam for a few days, I made the decision to change my way of life and become a Muslim, a follower of the Honarble Elijah Muhammad.

It was extremely difficult for me to tell my mother and the rest of my family about my decision to convert to Islam. To my utter amazement my mother was surprisingly calm about my decision, and didn't make a big deal of it. (I really should have realized that mother was praying hard for me). I suspect that my mother was very hurt by my decision, but she never let on that she was. It was Joyce, my sister who really grilled me hard about my decision, but I was determined that no one would influence me to change my mind. My mother continued treating me as though nothing had changed between her and I. She never made me feel ashamed in her presence.

The first time I visited the Mosque upon becoming a Muslim was an entirely different experience from just attending church. Converting to Islam meant that I had to adapt a whole new identity. This adaptation started with me changing my physical attire. I stopped wearing miniskirts and tight fitting jeans and started wearing long skirts, the length of which went down to the top of my shoes. And from then on, whenever I went outdoors I wore a scarf on my head. As soon as I entered the Mosque, before entering the fellowship hall, I was searched by a Muslim woman. This experience wasn't at all like going into the house of God where you just walked in without being searched, and you were accepted just as you are. The Nation of Islam changed my name from Linda Hall to Linda 50x. They taught all of us that our given names were slave names given to us by the white man who was the blue eyed devil. And now we had to renounce everything that we had learned from him.

My level of commitment to the Nation became greater the more I learned about Islam. I was seeing my new friend all of the time now, and I didn't feel depressed anymore. I stopped drinking and smoking cigarettes. I had finally found someone and something to live for. For the first time in a long time I really felt clean. I completely changed my diet. The Nation taught that we shouldn't eat pork. So, I abandoned my love for pork and bacon. We were also forbidden to consume white flour, sugar, and white bread. It made me feel as though the diet that I had eaten all of my life was the worst food that I could have ever put into my body. Ironically, everything that I was taught concerning the white man and the hatred that they had for him never diminished the respect I had for Mr. Hugh Jones who just happened to have bright blue eyes.

My family never rejected me. And although I made many attempts to convert a few of them, they made it plain to me that they would never convert to Islam. The Nation had a news publication called *Muhammad Speaks* that I started reading on a regular basis. I began learning about the movement called the Nation of Islam. Attending services at the mosque was totally different from going to church. What they taught at the mosque was so strange and different from what I was used to learning in church. And the seating arrangement in the mosque was totally different from the one in church. In church we all sat together, both male and female. In the mosque the men and women were separated from one another. On one occasion they taught us about how Elijah Muhammad became the leader of the Nation of Islam. Elijah Muhammad was originally Elijah Poole, a Baptist minister who had become a convert to Islam. Although I was an avid devotee of my new religion, I knew that most of their teachings didn't make any logical sense to me. One evening they told us that back in 1933 this Baptist minister, Elijah Poole had met this man who was a prophet. His name was Fared Muhammad. A group called the Black Muslims was formed out of this relationship. Fared Muhammad taught Elijah Poole (now Elijah Muhammad) that a scientist named Yakub had revealed to him that the White man was originally grafted from the Black man. As I continued my sojourn in the Nation, I started distancing myself from my family, and hanging out with my boyfriend Rodney who had recently become my fiance'. I started spending the night with him on the weekends, and on some weekdays also. Although I had divested myself from my former lifestyle, I still hadn't given up indulging in promiscuity.

However, even as I slept in his bed, deep in my heart I knew it was wrong for me to do so. I convinced myself that since I had stopped doing all of that other stuff, I would allow myself this indulgence, but in all reality I was operating in my own deception. As I continued attending the mosque I met a very nice young woman named Laura. Laura was in a romantic relationship with Rodney's best friend who was also a member of the Nation. Laura treated me very well. One day she offered to make me an entirely new wardrobe of long skirts that covered my whole body. She even made me a white uniform complete with the Fruit of Islam hat. This outfit was uniformly worn by all Muslim women every Sunday. Once a month Laura and I attended the women's class at the mosque. After class we would go out to eat at the Shabazz Restaurant on 116th in Manhattan's Harlem. The food in this place was so good that I began to collect recipes that I could fix at home. I learned how to make a few of their very tasty dishes, such as fish loaf and carrot cake. I made these dishes for my family and they loved them. In fact, my mother said that since I'd been eating such a healthy diet I ought to continue doing so. Very often I would eat dinner at Rodney's house. One week we would have vegetables with bean soup, and whole wheat bread. The next week we would have imported fish loaf from H&G Whiting. We only drank natural juices and I made sure that whenever I went shopping I didn't buy any foods that contain animal fats, white sugar, and breads.

In the late spring of 1975 Rodney invited me to go along with him and his best friend and his girlfriend Laura to spend a weekend in Connecticut. Rodney's friend's parents owned a summer home there. When we arrived at our destination, we went food shopping in order to stock up for our stay. One of the things we did that I really enjoyed was when we went bike riding. The place where we rode was so peaceful and quiet. It was wonderful. Later that night after going to bed, Rodney tried to have sex with me, but, even though I really didn't know why, I just couldn't do it.

After having dated Rodney for a few months, one day, while we were at his parent's home, he asked me to marry him. So, because I'd always dreamed of being a wife someday, I accepted. Of course, I was really excited about my engagement, but when I told my mother about it, her excitement was rather mollified. I started making wedding plans. I bought pots, pans, and dish sets. Laura and I spoke about how she would make my wedding dress. My commitment to Rodney and the Nation was complete.

As I was preparing to go to the mosque one Sunday morning, (my elder brother Vernon, who was living with our mother at the time, and preparing to go to church himself), challenged me. We were all sitting in Mother's beauty parlor when suddenly Vernon, catching me off guard, asked me what I was learning in the mosque. I knew that I couldn't give him an intelligent answer, because what was being taught was literally unintelligible to me. Most of what was being taught sounded ridiculous to my intellect. However, I continued in my own self deception. Rodney bought me a Quran, which the Muslims assert is their bible. I immediately began reading it voraciously. I was anxious to learn all that I could about Allah. But as I read the Book of Genesis in the Quran I discovered that it was totally different from the original version that I read in the Holy Bible. I was so consumed with learning about my newfound religion that I found myself purchasing other islamic books by a variety of authors. One day Rodney came by and suggested that I should legally change my name to an Islamic one. I chose the name Ameenah, and he agreed to it. After I told my mother about my name change, She simply responded with "Do what you want. I know what I named you." And she just left it at that. True to her words, she never stopped calling me the name that she gave me. My family always referred to me by my birth name. Linda Diane. But I always referred to myself as Ameenah.

Not long after Rodney and I were engaged, I began to have strange thoughts. I continued to communicate with my family, and I maintained a good relationship with them. I even attended St. James Holiness Church on some Sundays. On one occasion I went to one of my nephew's christening ceremonies. However, unbeknownst to me, my conflicting thought processes began taking a serious toll on my mental health. I started distancing myself from my family, especially my mother. I locked myself in my room, staying away from everyone. I continued reading and studying my Islamic materials, only coming out of my room to eat. Preparing my own food, I wouldn't eat any of the food that my mother prepared, or use any of her cooking utensils. This condition, or disposition is very hard to describe, but I started feeling alienated from all that I understood to be true prior to my convertion to Islam. And I was beginning to experience another conflict in my thoughts. Mr. Hugh Jones kept reaching out to me, even attempting to visit me. But I couldn't allow him to. However, I knew deep down in my innermost self that Mr. Jones had been and still was a dear friend to me. I found it to be extremely difficult to believe or accept any of the hateful things that they were saying about all white people. After all, Mr Jones was a white man who had beautiful blue eyes. My biological father was sick with lung cancer during this period of time, and was in Harlem Hospital. One day, while visiting with him, he literally begged me to leave the Nation of Islam. He explained to me that Elijah Muhammad was a corrupt influence in my life, and that I had really joined a cult. Although I maintained a healthy respect for my father, I refused to believe what he was saying to me and I continued to be stubbornly committed to my allegiance to the Nation of Islam.

One day my eldest brother Aaron, on his way home from work, stopped by Mother's house to see me. After hearing him knock on my bedroom door, I opened it, but when I saw that it was him, I refused to let him in. I told him that I didn't want to hear anything he had to say. At that moment I began to question my own sanity. I'd never had this kind of experience before. Who was this girl? I began to feel as if I was seeing myself outside of my own body. In reality, although I didn't realize it at the time, I was gradually beginning to lose control of my mind. As my behavior slowly began to change, my mother started to worry about me. She understood that I had converted to Islam, but now she began witnessing my slow mental demise, she desperately needed to know what was happening to me. She quickly enlisted my sister Joyce's help, asking her to take me to the doctor's office. I made an appointment to see a gynecologist who I knew and had worked for a few years earlier. His name was Dr. Cohen, and his office was in Manhattan. After finishing his examination, he called me back into his office and informed me that I was pregnant. Well, that diagnosis just blew my mind!!! I was completely stunned as I walked back out of his office into the waiting room where Joyce was waiting for me. I had no idea how I was going to explain to my sister that I was still sexually active.

Joyce was completely surprised when I told her that I was pregnant. She thought that I had been celibate since my conversion to

Islam. Rodney came by the house to see me, and I told him what my visit with the Dr. had revealed to me, and as soon as I stated that the doctor had informed me that I was pregnant his immediate reaction was one of stunned disappointment. He acted not only as if he was surprised, but he was terribly angry. I thought lo myself; Well, what did he expect? It is true that he told me that I shouldn't get pregnant, but we were having sex without any protection. His real fear was what the brother ministers would think and say about him. He didn't consider how I felt, or even show any concern for me at all. However, there was one thing that I had made up my mind not to do. And that was aborting this baby. The way Rodney conducted himself reminded me of how Norman responded to the same news. Although in comparison, I must admit that Norman's reaction wasn't nearly as hostile as Rodney's. His attitude toward me began to change almost immediately. He stopped coming to see me as much as he used to. And as a result, my feelings toward him started to change also. In fact, whenever we saw each other, it became very difficult for me to interact with him.

And then something really different started happening to me. I began hearing voices, and feeling as though people were plotting against me. In my mind I could hear them saying negative things about me. I was beginning to lose control over my own thoughts. It was as though an alien spirit had taken control of my mind. I started to withdraw within myself, and a deep depression began to characterize my emotional state. I couldn't fall asleep, and I stopped eating. I started to descend into a very deep and dark place, and I began to fear that this was a place from which I couldn't escape. My final break with reality happened after I heard the voices directing me to the mosque. I called a taxi, and waited in my room upstairs to hear the horn blow signaling that the taxi had arrived. It was the summer of 1975.

As I started to leave my room, my mother, whose room was adjacent to mine, started coming out of her room at the same time. As soon as I saw her, I was so terrified by her presence that I started screaming and ran down the stairs out of the door to the taxi waiting for me outside. Once I was in the cab I felt as though all rationality had abandoned me, and I completely lost control of myself. I felt like I was in a nightmare, on one of the worst acid trips that I had ever taken. Years before joining the Nation, I had indulged myself in an LSD foray, a drug that I swore that I would never use again, especially after seeing my then boyfriend and his friends take some. The day this happened, I was supposed to be at work. But I asked my sister Joyce to call me out sick. My mother and elder brother Vernon had gone grocery shopping and left me at home alone hallucinating (tripping). I certainly didn't want them to see me in that state when they returned, so I decided to go to work.

When I got on the train to Manhattan I was tripping so hard that I began seeing the faces of the people in the car start to fade away right before my eyes. I remember making it to the building where I worked, but have no memory of getting to my desk. I do remember feeling like I was typing one sentence for hours. This was the exact feeling that I had on my way to the mosque in the taxi cab. I was on a trip that I wasn't in control of. I gave the driver the address to the mosque on Bedford Avenue, and instructed him to take me there. I was obviously in a delusional state when we arrived at the mosque, and was immediately escorted away by two of the ministers at the entrance to the mosque. As I was standing on Bedford Avenue, I flagged down another cab. By now I had determined that I would go to the mosque on 116th Street in Manhattan. I was feeling as if I was in a daze, like I was on some type of drugs. I was determined to let the ministers at the main mosque know how I was so rudely treated at the mosque in Brooklyn. While I was In the cab, I began to disrobe, taking off all of my clothing. I vaguely remember leaving the cab with no clothing on at all. I started running down the block, but fortunately for me, the cab driver had already determined that something was wrong with me, and called the police. I believed that I must have blacked out by then, because the next thing that I remember was being on the psych ward at Kings County Hospital.

I remember going on a tour of Kings County Psychiatric Hospital while training to become a nursing assistant in high school. Now here I was, being admitted as a patient to their psych ward. I felt downright humiliated as I heard one of the officers say that a

50

great deal of young people from the Nation of Islam end up getting admitted to the psych ward at Kings County.

At this point in my life, I was no longer the woman that I thought I was. I felt hopeless, and now this strange place had become my home. I couldn't believe that I might be crazy also. It was a devastating shock for me to find myself sitting in a waiting room full of strange and crazy people who had lost their minds. To this day it remains a mystery to me of how the police found and reunited me with my family. During this period of time there were no cell phones, and, after leaving church, my mother had gone to the White Castle restaurant. After being admitted, I was taken up to one of the units and assigned a room. One of the nursing attendants brought me out into a large waiting room where my family was waiting to see me. All of my family, including the in-laws came to see about me. However, for some reason, based on what the voices were telling me, I didn't want to see my mother. The voices kept telling me that my mother was my enemy, but that was far from the truth. In reality I knew that my mother loved me very much, but I had succumbed to the insanity that was plaguing my mind. Everyone was there. My four brothers, and my sister Joyce. They all had come to see me. However, the only one that I could remember speaking to me was Aaron. In my incoherent state I kept calling him Dad. When they finally left, my brother Vernon was the last one to leave, and as he waved goodbye to me I could see the tears running down his face. I knew that it was extremely difficult for my family to witness my mental breakdown as they walked away through the electronic doors. One of the nurses had to force me to take my medications. What in the world was happening to me!!!??? I was struggling to maintain my own thoughts. It was as if all of my thoughts became a jumbled mess, and none of them made any sense to me. The voices were telling me that everyone I saw perspiring was a demon, therefore I must avoid them. The next day (which was Saturday), Rodney came to see me. And as he sat down next to me I could see great drops of sweat cascading down his face. He told me that I had to get well, and come home, because we were getting married, and our wedding was to take place that summer. I don't know how I responded, but after that, he never came back again.

While I was a patient at Kings County Hospital my maternal grandmother Mrs. Daisy Moore passed away. I don't know how, but I already knew that she died before anyone told me. I loved my grandmother. I remember her spending one summer with us when we lived in the Bronx. During that summer Grandma kept us while my mother went to work. Every Friday she would make soup and sandwiches for us, and she would watch all of our favorite TV shows with us. She was also a huge fan of soap operas, and she hated it when the TV commercials would interrupt her shows. Grandma also liked to dip snuff. She was in her eighties and living in a nursing home in Portsmouth Virginia when she died. With the exception of one of my siblings and myself, my entire family went to my grandmother's funeral. After having been mistreated at Kings County Hospital, it was either Aaron or Joyce who stayed with me in order to make sure that I was being properly cared for. Eventually Aaron was the one who found a more suitable environment for me. I was admitted to the psych ward in Methodist Hospital in Brooklyn. This ward had rooms that were better suited to my needs. There were only two patients assigned to a room and the staff seemed to be better organized than the staff at Kings County.

It was very strange for me to be in this place, away from home. This was a place where the patients walked around, and looked like zombies. And now I was also one of those patients. Joyce did a very good job helping me to settle in. She bought me my clothes (all of the patients had to wear our regular street clothes) and toiletries. During that period of my life, I continued to refer to myself as Ameenah. I still felt as though Islam was a part of my life. Joyce came to see me everyday. Each and every time she came through those locked doors I would be so happy to see her. It didn't take too long for me to ask to see my mother. My request was immediately granted, and when she came to see me, I was so elated to see her that my face broke out into a great big smile. My mother had always been there for me and now, when I needed her the most, I knew that she would be there for me. As soon as my mother came to see me, she removed the headscarf that I wore, and gave me a nice short wig. My mother was a skilled beautician and had a wonderful way of making you look beautiful, even though on the inside I didn't feel that way. Gradually, as time passed, I resumed the bad habit of smoking cigarettes. Actually all of the patients on the unit smoked, and we all had to report to the nurses station to get our medications. I would try my best to walk normally, but I always felt as though I was walking like the Frankenstein monster.

A psychologist named Dr. Sadegapor was assigned to my case, and told my mother that I was diagnosed to have an illness called Paranoid Schizophrenia. This illness is what caused me to have a complete nervous breakdown, hearing voices, and becoming delusional. During our sessions, Dr. Sadegapor would always ask me if I was still hearing the voices, but I wasn't at all sure of anything that I was hearing, because the psychotropic drugs they were injecting me with seriously impaired my judgment. And although I made valiant attempts to answer his questions, I had already determined that no one would ever know my deepest and darkest secrets. They were mine. and I had lo keep them to myself. However, having this attitude made it very difficult for him to help me. Everyday my mother would visit me. Whenever her schedule wouldn't allow her to, she always sent my sister Joyce to come and see about me. I was always happy when visitors came to see me. Visitations served to be an excellent distraction from the reality of the negative direction my life had taken. It was very difficult for me to face the reality of what really happened to me. Because of the wrong choices that I made in my life's experience I was now suffering from a nervous breakdown. I had totally succumbed to an anti-reality, and in all actuality had believed a lie. Although I was given sleep medication most nights, it was still very hard for me to fall asleep. During the day we would leave our rooms and participate in the various physical, and occupational therapies designed for us along with sessions with our assigned psychologists. Every Thursday we ate lunch with the staff and psychiatrists. This allowed the patients to socially interact with the staff and each other. I loved singing, and would sing Stevie Wonder's song "Love's in Need of Love," and John Denver's "Sunshine on My Shoulders

Makes Me Happy." The food that was served was catered and I really enjoyed eating it. Prior to the breakdown, I had lost a considerable amount of weight. However, after I started eating again I started to gain a few pounds.

One day my very best friend in the Nation came to see me. As we sat in the lounge, she appeared to be apprehensive. Laura had always been a good friend to me. However, I began to get the feeling that she wanted to say something to me, but was nervous about how I might respond. Finally, after trying to figure out how to say what she needed to say, she blurted out that Rodney and her sister were going to get married. Upon hearing that my fiance was to be married to someone else, I felt as if a stampeding herd of elephants had just trampled over my heart. I was so devastated that I found it hard to catch my breath, and I was at a complete loss for words. This was absolutely unbelievable. It hadn't even been a month since my breakdown, and Rodney was already planning to marry someone else!!! I was so hurt by Rodney's betrayal that I went into a deeper depression. I had planned my whole life around him, and now he was going to marry my best friend's sister. Everything that I had put my faith in was being destroyed right before me. I felt as if my entire life had been shattered into a million pieces. It felt as if it was more than I could bear.

After about a month, Dr. Sadegapor permitted me to go home on a weekend pass. He wanted my mother to determine how I conducted myself among my family. On the weekend of my return was my twenty second birthday. My mother brought me home in a taxi, but when I exited the car, everything looked so strange. It was as if I was entering a totally new environment.

As soon as I went into the house, I went to my room. My mother had spruced up my room. She bought new curtains for the windows and a new bedspread. Joyce had come over with her two children, Darryl and Chauntele. My Pops was there also, and although I was very happy to see him, there was still something missing. I didn't feel like myself. I was still very depressed, and most of the time I just stayed in my room. I would only leave my room when it was time to eat. My mother did everything in her power to make me feel comfortable. My birthday was on Sunday, and my mother had invited all of my brothers and their wives over to dinner to celebrate my birthday with me. However, I felt as if I was a stranger to the family that I grew up with, and who loved me. I started asking myself; how was I going to come back from this long journey? Would I ever recover from this mental breakdown?

While my mother and siblings were in the Kitchen, I was sitting down in my mother's beauty parlor looking out of the window, thinking how strange the block that I grew up on looked, when I saw Rodney strolling toward our house. At that moment, I was both surprised and happy to see him, and as he drew nearer, I began to perk up. When he rang the doorbell, I let him in and as he greeted me I sensed that something was up. I was still wearing the engagement ring that he had given me, and I thought that he might have come to tell me that what I had been told about him and Laura's sister wasn't true, that he still intended to marry me. But to my utter surprise, amazement and disappointment he had actually come by to ask me to return the ring to him. He informed me that his parents had paid for the ring and they wanted it back so that they could get a refund for it. I always thought that he had purchased it, but according to him, I was mistaken. He said that since we weren't getting married now, he needed me to give it back to him. I was absolutely devastated by this announcement, and thought to myself; Is this how you're going to leave the girl you professed to love for almost a year? As he left, I felt as if my heart had been torn to shreds. I had built my entire existence around being married to him, and now I had to face the reality that my marriage wasn't going to happen. At that moment I didn't think I had anything to live for. No longer was I the happy-go-lucky Linda Diane with the bright smile anymore. I also had to endure the fact that my family was a constant witness to my devastation after the breakup of my engagement.

On the Monday immediately after my birthday, (although a part of me really hated being there), I felt happy returning to Methodist Hospital. After what happened with Rodney, I began to feel like I might be better suited for that world now. It took weeks before I was discharged for good. One evening I was able to ask one of the nurses who was distributing medication what happened to me. She told me that the cause of my having a complete nervous breakdown was due to a lack of oxygen in my brain. Dr. Sadegapor told my mother that I would have to attend a rehabilitation center three times a week. And I would also have to talk to a psychologist twice a week.

Being back on the block just wasn't the same for me anymore. I was outside in my yard one afternoon when my former boyfriend Norman came out of his house, walking down the front stoop. He saw me and stopped to talk. He tried to reassure me that eventually I would feel better. I took the bus to both of my rehab and psych visits. The psych doctor couldn't really get anywhere with me, because when he questioned me about my past I would clam up and refuse to tell him anything. I wouldn't unlock the door to my mind in order to keep him out of my head. I did participate in arts and crafts at the rehab center, but I made sure to keep away from other people. One day during one of my sessions at the rehab center, I ran into a young man with whom I had gone to junior high school. I felt embarrassed having him see me there. I really didn't have any friends. I had managed to escape into my own world.

Even though I continued a regimen of sedatives and sleeping pills, I continued to be resistant to sleep. I stopped talking altogether, and just stayed in my room for hours, away from everyone. I wouldn't allow anyone into my word of silence. I kept all of my deep dark secrets locked up where I nor anyone else could find them. I became the little girl in the corner where it was safe to be all alone. I made sure that no one could enter the part of my life that I didn't want to confront. It was so much easier for me to retreat to the corner of my subconscious mind where the real Linda couldn't be found by anyone. I wasn't ready to be confronted by the demons that had acquired space in my head. There were too many of them. My mother had devoted herself to a constant prayer vigil for me. When she visited me she would pull me into her lap like she did when I was a little girl. There is truly nothing that is equal to a mother's love, especially when one is experiencing the true horrors of life.

Just before I experienced my first breakdown, I lost my biological father to lung cancer. My mother called me while I was at Rodny's house and informed me of my dad's passing. I was very surprised, because I knew he was sick, but I had no idea that he was literally dying. My brothers and sister Joyce all had gone to the hospital to see him the night before he passed, I was the only one that didn't go, and that really hurt me. I loved my father very much. Unfortunately it had taken years for him and I to develop a real relationship, and now he is gone at the young age of fifty five years old. When I told Rodney that my father died, he said that I must be the strong one in the family. He sounded as if he was saying that I shouldn' display any emotions. This was extremely difficult for me to do.

After getting off of the phone call with my mother, I wept bitterly at the loss of my father who I loved dearly. At his funeral I tried desperately to put on a brave face like my fiance requested me to do. Everyone of my father's living siblings and their families came to my mother's house for his funeral. All of my siblings and their families were there also. When it was my turn, I went up to my father's casket and looked at him for a few seconds. He looked like he was sleeping. I didn't allow myself to cry. Later on I suffered terribly for not allowing myself to grieve properly. I was glad that Pops had also come to the funeral.

Although my father wasn't a wealthy man in the material sense, he did manage to leave us an inheritance of land he and his siblings inherited from his parents. During the course of their marriage my mother had given birth to six children. All of us had been sired by the same man, and that man (my father) left the portion of his inheritance to his six children. In 1975, the year of my first nervous breakdown, my siblings and I were given a legal document offering each of us to sell our portion of the land. Unfortunately we all agreed to sell our inheritance. That was the one thing our father had left us. It was his legacy to us but in our ignorance we sold it. We should never have sold our inheritance, because no amount of money could ever equal the permanent value of our land. Years later, I would come to regret having agreed to selling what my father had given me. As a result of that very unwise decision my mother had to seek assistance from social services to take care of her now adult daughter. I was able to obtain medical benefits and food stamps in order to accommodate me now living at home with my mother.

During my stay at Methodist Hospital I was given a pregnancy test, which determined that I wasn't pregnant. Ironically I felt sad that I wasn't pregnant. But I realized that it would be impractical for me to dwell on it because I wasn't going to be married anyway. My family was very supportive of me. My sister Joyce became my very best friend. She did all that she could to get me out of myself imposed shell that I felt so safe in. She would come to my room and persuade me to go on errands with her. Whenever she saw that Mother needed a break, she would take me to her apartment on Tilden Avenue in Brooklyn. But I would only stay for a week at a time. I felt so out of place I found it enormously difficult to get through each day. I just couldn't feel like myself. I began to be overwhelmed by a feeling of never being able to return to any form of normalcy.

During one evening after returning home, I relapsed, and after I started hearing voices again, I had to be returned to Methodist Hospital. I found it easier to go back, because unfortunately, I had become accustomed to the environment. One day, my youngest brother Ronnie came to see me. He looked at me and observed that I was walking like the Frankkenstien monster in the movie. He insisted that I walk normally and kept trying to pull my hands down to my sides. Out of all of my siblings, Ronnie, who was the comedian of the family, was the one who could always make me laugh, no matter what I was going through. He and I were very close. My brother David also came to see me, but only once. His excuse was that he couldn't endure the smell of the perpetual odor of the hospital. He said that the odor caused him to feel sick, so he decided not to come back. My relapse was so severe that Dr. Sadegapor requested my mother allow him to give me a series of electric shock treatments. As they strapped me to the table, I remember being given an anesthetic that smelled like ether. Then probes were placed on the sides of my head that sent waves of electric shocks through my brain. This process was supposed to help bring me out of the severe depression that I was experiencing. My mother told me of an incident where I was attempting to climb the walls of the hospital. My illness was tearing her apart, and my family was desperately trying to get her to take a break from visiting me everyday. However, my mother's faith in God wouldn't allow her to give up on me. She believed with all of her heart that God would heal me from this dreaded disease.

During one of the sessions that my mother attended, Dr. Sadegapor suggested that my mother go with me to the mosque to see for herself what I was involved in. My mother's dedication to me prompted her to go with me. She wished to know the source of my distress. Her experience at the mosque made her feel very uncomfortable. She wasn't used to being searched from head to toe. As for myself, being in the mosque didn't feel the same anymore. However, I still tried to hold on to what I felt in the past with Rodney. One day, during an overnight visit with Joyce and her boyfriend Raymond, I was having a hard time falling asleep. I decided to go and lay down with Joyce and Raymond. He decided to try hypnosis on me in an attempt to get me to fall asleep. But it didn't work. I relapsed again, and was taken back to Methodist Hospital. This time I was so delusional that I had to be restrained in a straitjacket. I don't know how, but somehow I was able to get out of the restraints and I ended up being put in a padded cell that I called the quiet room. As for my mother, she, being driven by her faith along with one of my sister-in laws, went on a three day fast staying in the church building, praying for my deliverance. Finally, upon waking up I was suddenly inspired to sing a song that I had no way of knowing. The words to the song were; "There was a little girl in the corner. / Now she isn't there any longer. / She opened up her eyes and she let Christ reside./ There was a little girl in the comer."

Ironically, the acoustics in the cell were excellent, and the song sounded as if it came straight from heaven. Little did she know it at the time, but my mother's prayers had been answered. A little later on that day, I was released from the quiet room (padded cell), and allowed to return to my regular room. And when my mother came back to visit me, she was able to see the change in me that her prayers had wrought. I was back to myself.

After my return home I found it rather difficult readjusting to life on the outside. However, I did the best that I could under the circumstances. Late one night that summer, still wearing my Islamic garb. I went out into the front yard. I really wanted to feel like myself again, so I returned to drinking alcohol in the hope of feeling normal again. After some time had passed, I eventually returned to work part-time at the Medical Personnel Pool nursing agency.

One evening while I was in my front yard, I met a man, who, when he saw what I was wearing, hailed me with the Islamic salutation "As-salamu-alaykum." I returned his greeting and he introduced himself to me. His name was Brother Al. He stayed with me for a while and we talked. He requested my phone number, which I gave him, and after some time we began seeing each other.

During this period in my life I felt so lonely and I just wanted someone to be with. So, it wasn't long before I started going with Brother Al to his apartment and spending some nights with him. I felt that I needed to hold onto what I thought I had with Rodney. One day, while alone in his apartment, I found some love letters that had been written to him when he was in the Army. Naturally I questioned him about them, and he told me that they had been written to him by his ex-wife. I had never gone out with anyone that was married before, and I was very uncomfortable knowing that he had an ex-wife. However, he was able to convince me that his feelings for me were serious, but deep down in my heart I knew that he wasn't for me.

In addition to the job he had in the city, Al had opened a small business selling baked goods on the side. He requested me to manage the store, which was located on Fulton Street in downtown Brooklyn. I agreed to volunteer some of my time, and manage the store for him during the day, while he worked his fulltime job. Although I wasn't receiving a salary, working in the store did give me something to do, because I wasn't employed at the nursing agency during this period of my life. Al stocked his store with baked goods that he bought from a bakery outlet in Brooklyn. Every morning Al would pick me up at my home and drive me to the store, give me some cash for the register, and off he would go to work. I guess he trusted me to manage the store by myself. In general the store made good money, however there were days when the store didn't make much money, because hardly anyone came in. Eventually, Brother Al decided to close the store because it became economically insolvent and he couldn't make enough money to cover the overhead. I met Brother Al in the spring of 1976, and we broke up several months later.

There were times that I would attend church services with my mother, but my heart wasn't really into it. And sometimes my ex-fiance's mother would visit my mother, but I secretly knew that she was coming over to check on me. I believe that she wanted to see how I was doing after my breakup with her son. I would never allow her to see me sweat. I would ask her about her family and how they were doing. My dear friend Hugh Jones continued to call and ask me to marry him, but my answer to him was always no. It is so ironic to me that all my life I sought the love of a man, but in reality it was the love of my heavenly Father that I was really looking for.

One Saturday, while spending the weekend at my sister Joyce's house, I begged her to go out to the club with me. Joyce didn't know how to disco dance, and therefore it took me a long time to convince her to come with me that night. Personally, I loved going out clubbing. Dancing to the powerful disco music while the strobe lights were blinking on and off at a wonderfully fast pace gave me a feeling of exhilarating excitement. The discotheque was the place that I loved to hangout in. When I was a teenager a few of the young people who lived on my block would come to my house and we would practice doing the latest dances in my living room. That night Joyce and I caught a cab to a discotheque called "The Last Word." Before converting to Islam, this was the club I always went out to when I wanted to hangout. Before arriving at the club, Joyce and I had a few drinks. We went in and found our seats. As I sat down and my eyes began gazing around the great expanse of the dance floor, I caught sight of a young man dancing smoothly on his feet, not missing one beat. What really captured my attention was that while he was dancing with this young lady he was purposely staring into her eyes as he held her hands. I thought to myself; "Please let him ask me to dance." I thought that he was the best dancer in the room. He was doing a dance called "the Brooklyn Hustle." Finally he made his way to where my sister and I were seated and asked my sister to dance with him. I felt disappointed at first, but decided that I would wait patiently for my turn. Finally he extended his hand toward me and asked me to dance with him. My heart was pounding as I took hold of his hand. I really wasn't sure that I could keep up with him. That's how good he was. His dance steps were all original. They were like nothing I had ever seen before. I was surprised to see that I was able to keep up with his every move. I didn't miss one step. We were like Fred Astaire and Ginger Rogers. It was as though we had been dancing together all of our lives. After dancing for a while, he escorted me to the club's upstairs lounge, and we talked for several hours. During our conversation, he asked me for and I gave him my telephone number. The next Saturday I went to the club, hoping that I would see him, and I did.

The young man's name was William D. Carter, III. He informed me that I had given him the wrong number, but I assured him that I had given him the correct number, and told him that he must have written it down wrong. As we exchanged addresses, we learned that we lived directly across the street from each other. I lived at 698 Sterling Place and he lived with his mother at 717 Sterling Place. He told me that as he sat on the front stoop of his mother's building, he often saw a bright light on in my mom's beauty parlor. Of course he didn't know that it was her beauty parlor at the time, but was always attracted to the light that he saw in the window. He said that he was always wondering who lived in that house.

William and I started seeing each other every week, and then everyday. Not long after I decided to introduce him to my family. He would come to my house early in the morning and my mother would make us breakfast. One day, he came by the house, and he sang a song to me in front of my mother. The name of the song was "My Funny Valentine" by Dakota Staton. William was raised in Harlem, and the Bronx. His parents brought him up musically on Jazz. The song was so sweet that it impacted my mother to the point of her blushing. At the very beginning of our relationship I was honest with William, who preferred to be called Bill, and told him about my nervous breakdown. I decided not to keep such an important detail about myself from him. I truly believe that William and I were destined to be together. Especially since we both had lived in the Bronx at the same time. And now we lived directly across the street from one another. Our first meeting happened approximately around the July 4th holiday in 1976. Not too long after that we fell in love with one another. William took me across the street lo meet his mother and younger sister Althea. I would go over to his house and we would make love to each other in his room. Now I realized that I could no longer afford to just give myself to any man anymore. I had been looking for the man that I would spend the rest of my life with. William was different from any other man that I had been involved with. He loved me completely, faults and all. William had been looking for a job for a long time, and finally found one as a welder in the Brooklyn Navy Yard. Ironically my biological father had been a welder in the Portsmouth Naval Yard when we lived in Virginia.

As I continued working for the Medical Personnel Pool agency in my capacity as a nursing assistant, William and I had a whirlwind summer romance. At that time I was working with a family in the Jamaica Estates in Queens, New York. On some Friday evenings William would come over and stay with me until Saturday morning, and then he would ride home with me on the train. That evening before we left the next morning, I would make filet mignon and baked potatoes for dinner, and we would dine in the backyard of my patient's palatial estate. One Saturday morning after arriving home from work, my mother gave me a solemn warning. She told me that if I kept allowing William to come out to my job I would lose the assignment. Well, as usual my mother was right. One Saturday morning just as William and I were leaving to go home, Mr. Nemmett, my patient's son, was coming toward us, and as we walked out of the house, he greeted us and continued on into the house. A few days after that, the agency called and told me that I was no longer needed at that assignment.

William (who from now on will be referred to as Bill) had a brother named Dennis, who was a member of the Air Force. Dennis was home on leave and had come to visit their mother. Bill had invited me over to his mother's house to meet him. Unfortunately this was taking place just as I was beginning to get sick again. Once again I started not sleeping and I lost my appetite. These were definite signs that I was beginning to experience another breakdown. Because I wasn't eating or sleeping. I became paranoid and delusional. I tried with all of my might to fight against those horrible feelings that seemed to take over both my mind and body. I knew that I needed to be well so that I wouldn't embarrass Bill when I met his brother. When I got to Bill's mother's apartment, I had completely lost control over my thoughts, and, once again, I began to hear those horrid voices. As we all sat in his mother's kitchen, Althea, Bill's younger sister, facetiously said to Dennis "This is Bill's girlfriend, Linda." I knew that Bill was upset, but he was there for me. At that moment, Lydia, Bill's baby sister, went across the street to get my mother. When they returned, my mother took me home. I believe my mother had already discerned that I was breaking down again. The next morning my mother took me back to Methodist Hospital, my home away from home. Everyday, after coming home from work, Bill would come to the hospital to visit me. When I saw him coming down that long corridor I would be so happy to see him. He would always put a smile on my face. I had fallen in love with him, and I knew that this time it was real. I felt like I'd finally found someone who truly loved me. Bill's commitment to me in the midst of my breakdown proved to me beyond a shadow of a doubt that he really loved me also. I knew that I had found a special place in his heart.

When I met Bill for the first time, he was twenty seven years old. He was performing with a small group of actors called "The Ju-Ju Players" in a small theater at the "Henry Street Settlement" in lower Manhattan. During this period of his life he was a struggling actor. I watched him perform in a couple of plays. Bill was also pretty intelligent and could express himself well. He had been a student at Queens College a few years before we met. But Bill also had a dark past that he eventually told me about. He had been addicted to heroin earlier in his life, and was still smoking majuana, and using cocaine. I really didn't find it to be a problem for me at that time, because I was also using cocaine, smoking majuana, and drinking alcohol. There is one particular quality that Bill displayed that I really appreciated. He was always brutally honest about himself and with me. In my experience with the men that I had dealt with, honesty was a major rarity. None of them had ever been honest about their feelings toward me. After being discharged from the hospital I developed the habit of sitting on my stoop drinking beer and waiting for Bill to come home from work. He would round the corner from Franklin Avenue onto Sterling Place, and walk down the block toward my house. Once he got close our eyes would make contact, and he would wink at me. That gesture would just melt my heart. Bill would also tell me in no uncertain terms that he disliked me sitting on the stoop drinking beer.

Joyce knew that I was in love with Bill, because the walls in our bedroom were plastered with a lot of his portfolio pictures. She looked at me and said "Girl, you're crazy." One day, as we were sitting in my mother's beauty parlor, Joyce decided to see how much Bill loved me. The seats in the parlor were situated in such a way that they were placed close to one another. Joyce got up from her seat, came over to me, and took my shoes off of my feet and set them in Bill's lap. Then she turned to him and asked. "Do you really love my sister?" To which he replied "Yes, I do." Then Joyce looked at him and said "I'm glad, because you have to love these feet too." Well, as I'm sure that you can very well imagine. I had never been so embarrassed in my entire life. I had never exposed my feet to anyone, because I had allowed my vanity to get the best of me. I would always buy shoes that were really too small for my feet, because I wanted them to look cute. My sister had always warned me about doing that. but I wouldn't listen. And now my feet had been exposed to reality. In addition, no one in my family had the best genes when it came to feet. I was horrified. I thought to myself how could my own sister do this to me? However, I quickly recovered, because I was very pleased with Bill's response.

Soon after the "foot" incident, Bill moved out of his mother's apartment and into a rooming house on Madison Street, about three blocks from Sterling Place. I started spending some nights with him and in the morning when he left for work, I would return home. One morning, after I went home, my mother met me as I was coming into the front entrance of the house. She looked straight at me and gave me a two-choice ultimatum: either get married or move out. As I looked into her eyes, I knew that my mother was deadly serious, and it was time for me to make a decision in terms of what I intended to do. One evening, as we were standing at the bus stop on the corner of Bedford Avenue and Sterling Place, I asked Bill if he intended to marry me. He appeared to be shocked and surprised at the question. A few days later, Bill told me that he'd been looking for a wife for quite some time, and that since he knew that we loved each other we should get married. And although we really had no idea of what marriage was really about, and no one to advise us, we were married at City Hall in New York on April 27, 1977. The ceremony was a simple one, and our witnesses were both of our mothers. Later that year my mother arranged a church wedding for us, and we married again in the church that I grew up in on August 27, 1977. I wore a beautiful white wedding gown and hat, and Bill wore a white tuxedo with black trimming.

With the help of my sister's boyfriend Raymond, Bill found a one bedroom apartment in the Flatbush section of Brooklyn. The building was located on Campus Road, across the street from Brooklyn College. Because our furniture wasn't due to arrive until later on in the week, we had to borrow my bed from my bedroom in my mother's house to sleep on.

My brother Ronnie gave us a small black and white TV set for a wedding gift. We had a cozy little honeymoon for three days in our new apartment. I was so happy to be Mrs. William Carter. Bill had purchased two beautiful wedding rings for us. At this point in my life, I knew that Bill was the one that I'd been waiting for all of my life. I was just so sorry that I had allowed so many wrong men into my life before meeting the one that I would truly love and call my husband. Our refrigerator didn't arrive for several days. So we went out to eat at McDonald's restaurant every evening. I enjoyed strolling down the long block together with my new husband. We were so very much in love. And then, after three days of wedding bliss Bill had to return to work. The reality of what being a wife realty meant would now set in. I didn't have any formal training on how to be a wife with the exception of my mother's example, and the casual observances of other married couples. But I hadn't been given the very necessary information that I needed in order to know how to conduct myself like a married woman. I would stay in bed all day and get up in just enough time to prepare dinner for Bill before he got home from work. I was horribly ignorant in terms of knowing my role as a wife. If a woman is properly mentored in her youth, she will receive the necessary training that is needed to be a wife. But I wasn't afforded that type of opportunity, because my mother hadn't received it from her mother. Therefore she couldn't give me what she didn't have. It would be years later in our marriage, after learning the true significance of being a wife, that I would teach a class and relay this information to younger women who were preparing to be married.

It was during this period of time that Bill and I had our first knockdown dragout fight. Bill became violently angry with me, because I had mistakenly left one of his record albums on the steam radiator in our living room where it melted. Until this incident I had no idea that his temper could become this violent. Whenever he would anger me I would lash out at him, and he would respond by hitting me. Although I never fought him back, I would use my tongue to effectively antagonize him. My way of getting even with him was to shut off all verbal communication, and sexual activity. I knew that I could hurt him that way, and I did. But it wasn't doing our marriage any good. Bill would ultimately feel terrible after abusing me. He would cry and beg me to forgive him, and in spite of its distortion, this did give me a greater sense of his love for me. After all, I was very opinionated, and refused to see anyone's point of view except my own.

I eventually went back to work for the Medical Personnel Pool Nursing agency in the summer of 1977. I was given an assignment in a nursing home called Workmen's Circle, located in the Bronx. I worked the evening shift from 4:00pm until 12:00 midnight, and then I would take the train home. My mother had given me this book called Miracles of Healing. It was written by Evangelist Oral Roberts. As I read this book, I began to feel the LORD calling me, and my understanding began to open up to His miracles. On July 13th and 14th, the entire city of New York experienced an electrical blackout. I was at work and had to stay at the nursing home all night.

It was the first time that Bill and I were separated from each other. It took me an hour to get home by taxi the next day.

Having to adjust to one another was very difficult, and caused our arguments and fights to get worse. Bill would sincerely make valiant attempts to talk to me, but I would angrily and stubbornly shut down all avenues of communication. Simply put, I wouldn't talk to him, no matter how hard he tried. This response to his attempts infuriated him. What he didn't realize at that time was the fact that I never received physical discipline as a child, although my siblings did. Therefore it became very difficult for me to receive any corrections from him, especially concerning myself. I would deliberately provoke an argument, then watch him change from being a mild mannered person into a raging monster. There were times when I knew that if I were to say one wrong word to him I would provoke him into anger, but I would say it anyway. A lot of our fighting stemmed from the fact that I wouldn't be quiet, and I didn't know how to avoid confrontation. I began having murderous thoughts about my husband, and although I knew that I would never hurt him, these thoughts persisted. Although we loved each other, we had to learn how to live harmoniously with each other.

After living on Campus Road for almost a year somehow Bill got Into a verbal altercation with our landlord concerning late payment of the rent. During this altercation, Bill threatened him with physical harm, and in return we were sent an eviction notice. As a result we had to move all of our belongings into a storage unit somewhere in the Bronx. And then we moved into a very small bedroom in my mother's house. About two weeks later my brother David informed us that he knew of some vacancies in a housing project called the Vanderveer Estates. We successfully applied for and moved into a one bedroom apartment at 1414 New York Avenue. My sister Joyce pitched in and helped move our stuff out of storage into our new apartment in Flatbush Brooklyn. She also informed us that moving to our new place would be just like moving to Viet Nam.

I was very happy that we were able lo find another apartment so soon after being evicted from our Campus Road apartment. We bought a new dinette set, and I painted our bedroom burnt orange with a dark brown ceiling and framework. We had a platform bed that I put a burnt orange bedspread on with dark brown pillows. Our bedroom looked to me like a beautiful sunset. I had painted a beautifully romantic atmosphere. However, we had to deal with the rodent and insect problem, which I hated, and was horrified by. I would turn on the lights in the kitchen at night and see rodents running across the floor, and over my stove, and across the living room floor. This literally sent chills up my spine. We had to set traps and put down poison. I hated the smell of dead rats.

By 1978 I decided to continue my education, and enrolled in the Advanced Career Technical Center to become a lab technologist. Bill and I were still arguing and fighting. And not too long after enrolling in school I had my first breakdown while being married. I started feeling paranoid, hearing voices again, and would wake up screaming, frightening Bill out of his sleep. I would tell Bill that I was hearing people talking outside of our apartment. Of course Bill had no idea of how he would deal with me. After all, he was attempting to deal with his mentally disturbed wife. We were very young and uninformed and had no idea of how this issue would affect our marriage. My illness would have a negative affect on our marriage for the next few years. After about three years, Bill started seeing other women. He would always let them know that despite his being involved with them, he loved me, and would never leave me. But his infidelity really placed a rift in our relationship. One of the major contributing factors to his unfaithfulness was my refusal to make love to him. The first major affair that Bill had was with an older woman that one of his aunts introduced him to. I was quite aware that it was happening, but I refused to face the reality of my husband being romantically involved with someone else. I also found it very difficult to continue going to school, because I was always in and out of Methodist Hospital. Almost every other year, right around our anniversary. I would start breaking down. Dr. Sadegapor informed my mother that I would break down approximately every two years, and recommended that I continue taking my medication. But as soon as I started feeling better, I would become non-compliant.

While I was attending school, I met a young lady named Sandra Clark. We instantly became very good friends. About two or three months later, Sandra moved into an apartment where Bill and I lived with her three children. We visited each other. As we became more and more acquainted, I told Sandra about my experiences in the Nation of Islam and how being in the Nation had caused me to have a nervous breakdown. She herself had been a member of the Nation some years earlier, but was no longer involved with them. Sandra would come by the apartment on Fridays, and we'd sit down at the dining room table listening to music, talking, drinking beer, and smoking pot. Sometimes Joyce would come over also, and we all would hang out and socialize together. On one of these occassion, Joyce spontaneously broke out into a Gospel song called 'Going Up Yonder' by a Gospel group called 'The Hawkins Family.' Bill and I sang along with her. Joyce, who had given her life to the LORD when she was fourteen year old, was in a backslidden state, and had a drinking problem. However, it wouldn't be too long before she would give her life back to Him.

Whenever I broke down, Bill would always have to get someone to stay with and attend to me, because he had to work. He would invite my sister-in-law, Althea Taylor to stay with me whenever I was on the verge of breaking down. On one occasion in 1978, while I was attending Advanced Career Training, I suddenly became catatonic. I kept hearing the voices telling me not to speak. I kept trying to say something, but I felt like I was bound. The words were right there, but wouldn't come out of my mouth. Once again my mind shut down on me. My husband was able to get in touch with a couple of my classmates and requested that they come over to see me. I guess he thought that they might be able to get me out of the state of mind that I was in. However, in reality no one could help me. I needed the LORD to intervene on my behalf. I was going through something that only God Himself could get me out of. Bill recognized the symptoms of another breakdown, and although he hated it, he knew he had to take me back to the hospital. One day, while his mother was looking after me, upon his arrival from work, Bill had to forcibly take me to the hospital. I was kicking, screaming and cursing. Bill said to me some time later that he knew that it wasn't me, because I didn't use profanity. Bill faithfully came to see me everyday. I looked forward to seeing him come through those locked doors. He always put a smile on my face, because he would always display his signature of love and affirmation for me by winking at me.

On my twenty-fifth birthday Bill invited a few of our friends and family to celebrate with me. My mother-in-law bought me this beautiful gold necklace. Two of my siblings, David, and Joyce came over to help me celebrate. We did a lot of entertaining in our little apartment. Bill informed me that he was never celebrated when he was a child, so I arranged a big party for him every year. I would invite all of his friends and family over, and we would dance the night away.

On one of our celebrations Bill's father came to his party and celebrated with us. My girlfriends and family also attended. I also invited a really good childhood friend of mine named Kevin Johnson over, and he tended bar for us. My mother-in-law, and sister-in-law, who were both fantastic cooks prepared all of the food, and we had enough for everyone and then some. All in all I believe that was the best party that I ever threw for Bill.

Bill had been employed as a welder for Seatrain Shipbuilding at the Brooklyn Navy Yard. However, after losing his job he enrolled In PSI to study computer programming. He graduated from the school with an A+ average. And my brother Vernon was able to get him a job as a programmer for the company he worked for. But Bill didn't last long, because of a conflict that he had with his boss. As the years went by, our lives became more difficult. Sometimes we would attend church services with my mother. One Sunday my husband began to participate in the worship service, clapping his hands as the choir song. But I didn't wont to give my life to the LORD at that time, so I didn't participate. However, I didn't realize that the LORD was trying to get our attention. I believe that if someone had explained the message of the Gospel to us we might have given our lives to the LORD then. But the truth is that there was no one who could effectively impart the message to us. My mother, who was always there, continued to pray for us, and one day some years later, her prayers were answered.

Every Friday was the day when I would clean our apartment from top to bottom. My biological father was a clean fanatic, and he influenced me to develop a penchant for cleaning. Afterward I would go out to the corner grocery store at Foster and Nostrand Avenues to get a couple of quarts of Miller High Lite Beer. By the time Bill came home from work I had already been inebriated for quite some time. He in turn, would always bring home at least three record albums and a $5.00 bag of reefer. Sometimes we would also walk together to the liquor store on Nostrand Avenue and purchase a fifth of Smirnof vodka. During this period of our lives, Bill was working In the Wall Street distinct of Manhattan for an investment firm called A.G. Becker, and would get paid every Friday. Sandra, and our other good friend, Carol Simmons would come over, and we would get blasted, drinking alcohol and smoking pot. We would talk for hours. During one of these sessions, while Bill was talking to us, we all concluded that he should be a preacher. Little did we realize that the LORD had great plans for his life.

After a few years into our marriage I began seriously thinking about having children. I knew that the ectopic pregnancy that I had some years earlier could lessen my chances of getting pregnant, but I never believed that it would never happen for us. Back in 1975 my gynecologist informed me that I had a small ovarian cyst, but I wasn't to worry about it. When I began my quest to get pregnant, several gynecologists told me that I had developed fibroid tumors on my uterus, and most of them suggested that I have a hysterectomy, but I refused to do so. I continued to believe that Bill and I were going to have children, and I wouldn't allow anything, or anyone to deter me from that. On one of my visits to the doctor, I was given an examination called a Hysterosalpingogram. This is a test that is used to examine the cavity of the uterus and Fallopian tubes in order to see if they were blocked. I took the bus to the doctor's office without Bill, because he had to work. I never realized that the procedure would be so excruciatingly painful. The procedure revealed that I only had one functioning fallopian tube. The other one was buried deep under scar tissue, and wasn't functioning at all. Although the doctor didn't give me much hope, I wouldn't give up, and persisted on my quest. I went to a fertility specialist to see what could be done about my infertility. Now I began experiencing the consequences of the ungodly choices I had made. I began to look back and remember the babies that I killed as the memories of the abortions I had started to haunt me. It was extremely difficult for me to talk about what I was going through with my husband. All I knew is that I really wanted to have children. The few specialists who examined me left me little hope that I would ever get pregnant. The only hope that I needed to rely on would come from the LORD. I needed a miracle from God.

Now my marriage was in real trouble. Bill was selling pot and was smoking it everyday. He was also hanging out with some really shady people who I didn't approve of. We were fighting at a much greater frequency than before. I would have scars on my face from his physical abuse, scars that I couldn't explain to my family when I visited them. When my sister Joyce would come over, I would attempt to hide the bruises on my face from her by wearing dark glasses, but Joyce always knew what happened. I was also returning to Methodist Hospital every two years. My situation became so bad that I would find myself sitting in my bedroom alone, talking to my dead babies. I would have entire conversation with them, talking with them as though they were with me in the room. I created a make believe world that I thought that I was in control of. One day, Bill came home from work and found me trying to climb out of our bedroom window. The voices had told me that I was "Wonder Woman," a fictional character played by the actress Lynda Carter. The voices convinced me that I could fly. I was a psychological wreck that needed more than psychological and medical attention. I needed a miracle from God.

One day, while I was visiting my mother-in-law, I heard someone call me three times by my middle name, "Diane, Diane, Diane." I looked around to see who was calling me, and I didn't see anyone. Before getting on the bus on the way home, I went to the grocery store on the corner of Bedford Avenue and Sterling Place. After getting home. later that night Joyce called us to let us know that a young 14 year girl named Diane had been shot dead in the same store that I went to earlier that day. At that point, I knew that the LORD was calling me, and I got down on bended knee and repeated the Sinner's prayer. However, because I didn't really understand the seriousness of what I'd done, I ended up going back to my old lifestyle.

Soon after this happened, my mother invited me to her weekly Bible study. She told me that she had invited a young minister over to teach the class. My friend Sandra and I decided to go. The minister had been a drug addict and dealer before his conversion. He testified how he had given his life to the LORD and how the LORD had delivered him from a life of drug addiction and crime. His testimony convinced both Sandra and myself to repent and give our lives to the LORD. I was 'born again' on May 2nd, 1982, and my life has never been the same since that night. While it took some time before I stopped smoking cigarettes, I was able to quit every one of my other bad habits immediately. I instantly knew that I had changed. I knew that the LORD had forgiven all of the horrible choices that I'd made, and all of the terrible sins I'd committed. I had a brand new life and a brand new beginning. This feeling was nothing like I felt in the Nation of Islam. No, this feeling was real. I had finally met the real true and living God, and HIS name was Jesus Christ, the SON of the living God. From then on Sandra and I went to my mother's Bible study every Monday evening. I also began attending church service habitually. Sometimes Bill would tell me to stay at home, and I would comply, but he always went out after awhile. I never preached to Bill. I simply tried to live the life of a true believer before him as best as I could. My final visit to Methodist Hospital was in 1983. Dr. Sadegapor had told both my mother and my husband that I would always suffer mental illness, and that I would continue to have breakdowns every two years. It has been thirty-six years since I was healed from paranoid schizophrenia, and I give all the praise and glory to the Lord Jesus Christ, the Savior of my soul.

I needed to go back to work, so I took an assignment with the New York City Home Health Agency. Fortunately, I was able to work for a young lady named Audrey Greenfield. She was the niece of one of the members of St. James Holiness Church. Audrey was a type 1 diabetic. She had been declared legally blind and had already had one leg amputated. In addition to that, both of Audrey's parents had died of diabetes. I would alternate between twelve-hour shifts. One week I worked the 7:00 a.m. to 7:00 p.m. shift, and the next week I worked the 7:00 p.m. to 7:00 a.m. shift. The assignment paid well, and God knows Bill and I needed the money. Bill had acquired his security guard certification, and worked at our apartment complex for SSI Security as a security officer.

One week after working the 7:00 a.m. to 7:00 p.m. shift. I came home, and as I opened the door, because of the way our apartment was designed, I could see a young lady sitting on the toilet in our bathroom. As soon as she saw me, she immediately exited the apartment. I certainly didn't want to believe that my husband and this woman were having sex in our bedroom, but all evidence to the contrary was there. As you can imagine I was livid with anger as I questioned my husband why this woman was in our apartment. He gave me some lame excuse. And based on my recent conversion to Christ, I couldn't remain angry with him. I concluded that the only way to save my marriage was to put it in the hands of God. Bill was living a terrible lifestyle. Although he continued working his day job, he also had a night job as a bouncer in an after hours club. I had warned him that if I discovered that he had a gun in our home I would leave him. One day while I was cleaning our bedroom I found his gun in his night stand drawer. I immediately packed my belongings and moved back in with my parents. I knew that fixing our marriage was beyond my control. I also realized that the wedding vows we took included the words "for better or for worse." However I also knew that I couldn't back down on my word to leave if I found a gun in our home. Besides, I was not going to be the "sacrificial lamb." Everyday Bill called me, begging me to come back. But I knew that I couldn't. I wanted to, and would find excuses to do so… I would tell him that I needed to water my plants, and when I would visit him I observed that he was getting worse. He had lost a tremendous amount of weight, and was starting to look bad. I still loved my husband, but all I could do for him was pray for him. My mother continually advised me to put him in the hands of God, but I found it extremely hard to do.

I took great pleasure in taking care of Audrey Greenfield, a Type 1 diabetic. Sometimes I would take her to church with me on Sundays. I would read the Bible to her everyday. Every Sunday evening Audrey and I would watch "A Study in The Word " with Jimmy Swaggart, I loved to hear him teach God's Word. I had fallen in love with God and I simply couldn't get enough of Him. Every evening after putting Audrey to bed, I read my Bible. I discovered that I had a tremendous hunger for God's Word. Audrey was also on dialysis and had to go to the dialysis unit in Far Rockaway three times a week. Audrey loved to eat corned beef sandwiches from the deli. She and I had some really great times together. She was a delightful person and a very good friend. In the summer of 1983, Audrey was hospitalized at Kings County Hospital, because her blood sugar level had become hyperglycemic. After being discharged, she requested that I buy her a corned beef sandwich before going to dialysis, After arriving at the dialysis unit, I gave her half of the sandwich, and told her she could have the other half after she completed dialysis. To my shock and great disappointment Audrey coded on the dialysis machine and later died at a nearby hospital. I was heartbroken when the doctor came into the waiting room and told me that Audrey didn't make it. I lost a very dear friend and a sister in Christ. Now I had the very unpleasant duty of letting her aunt. (Sister Mary Pierce) know that Audrey had died. When I called her she instructed me to take a taxi to her house and she would pay for it. I was crying profusely as I rode home alone in the taxi. I was so devastated by Audrey's passing that I couldn't attend her funeral. Audrey's sudden death was just too much for me at the time.

One day, our good friend, Carol Simmons called me at my mother's house. She informed me that Bill needed something to eat and she was unable to get it for him. I bought him some Chinese takeout, got in a cab and took it to him. Once I got into our apartment I started desiring my husband. He came up behind me and cornered me while I was in the bathroom. I immediately felt a rush of heat crash all over my body and I knew that I had to get out of there fast. Making love to him at that time wouldn't fix our marriage. Soon after, to my complete surprise, Bill called me, and asked me for a divorce. I knew that we loved each other, and had something special. I called my pastor who suggested that we hold off on divorce and get a legal separation for now. But I really didn't want a divorce. I began praying earnestly for my husband's salvation. I knew that this kind of love connection only came around once in a lifetime.

A little while after Audrey's death, my mother took me with her on vacation along with Joyce's two children Darryl and Chauntele, and my adopted brother and two sisters to Wildwood New Jersey. She managed to get enough beds for all of us to stay in the same room at the same hotel. I had a huge amount of fun with the children and my mother. Wildwood Park was a resort area that had an amusement park. We would walk on the boardwalk and go to the amusement park everyday. We rode the trolley cars in order to get to the board-walk. I hadn't had fun like that in a very long lime. I decided to send my husband a postcard, but I later learned that he was angry because he thought that I was flaunting our separation in his face. But I had no intention of hurting his feelings. I just wanted lo let him know that I was thinking about him.

I learned to embrace the LORD with all of my heart. I had developed a strong prayer life, and I went to church services as often as I could. On the final day of the vacation as I was lying in bed, I started to think about Bill, and my heart longed for him. It was kind of weird, because now that I loved the LORD, HE was lead-ing me back to my husband and showing me that I still loved him. On the way back to Brooklyn, I thought about Bill the entire trip home. That Saturday evening I called my best friend Sandra, and she requested that I meet her at Carol's apartment. After I arrived, they invited me to spend the night with them. I accepted, and we had a wonderful time talking, laughing, eating and reminiscing.

During our conversation, as we were sitting there, with her eyes gleaming, Carol said to me "Guess who's going to church with me tomorrow?" Who? I responded. She replied "Billy" (she always called him Billy). She wanted Sandra and I to meet her at the church, because Bill was still angry with me about the postcard that I sent him. She thought that if Bill knew that I was going to be there, he might not go. That Sunday morning, Sandra and I took the bus to Brooklyn Miracle Temple on Bedford Avenue. As I sat down in my seat, I would occasionally glance at the back door to see if Carol and Bill had arrived. As soon as I saw him come in, I turned my head. I didn't want to take the chance of him seeing me and walking out. The minister read from the book of Philippians chapter 3, verse 13. "Brethren, I count not myself to have apprehended: Forgetting those things that are behind, and reaching forth unto those things that are before." After he spoke, he made an altar call and asked everyone to bow their heads and close their eyes. As I sat there with my eyes closed, I prayed, "Father God, please save my husband. Please let him be at the altar when I open my eyes."

I listened as the minister recited the "Sinner's" prayer to those who had accepted his invitation to the altar. And when I lifted my head and looked toward the altar, I saw my precious husband standing there hugging the man of God with a strong embrace. My prayer had been answered. My husband had repented and given his life to the LORD. My heart literally leaped for joy. After the benediction at the end of the service, I went over to where Bill was seated and congratulated him upon his new birth and becoming a new creation in Jesus Christ. He was a little distant, but that was okay, because I knew that the LORD had given him a brand new life with a brand new beginning. And for that I would always be eternally grateful. Another close friend of mine named Corrie, was rather disappointed that I didn't display as much excitement for Bill's conversion as she did. However, she didn't understand that inwardly I was literally overwhelmed with joy, to the point of being practically speechless. When we got back to my mother's house, she was in the front yard sitting in her lounge chair. As soon as I told her that Bill had given his life to the LORD she jumped out of her seat and started praising God with all of her strength, thanking Him for her son-in-law's new birth.

Not long after giving his life to the LORD, Bill called me and asked me to forgive him for the way he had treated me. I in turn asked for his forgiveness. For many of our years together I thought that I was the only one being hurt. But in reality, I knew that I had to face the fact that I also had contributed mightily to the collapse of our marriage. One afternoon, before I went to work, I went to see Bill, and as we fully returned ourselves to one another, we talked and made glorious love together. We both knew that our love for each other remained strong. The forces of evil had failed in their attempt to break us apart, and now we were truly bound together and were as strong as a threefold cord (Eccl. 4:12). It had been a long time since I'd been in the arms of my husband, and we spent a wonderful afternoon together. We had so much to talk about. I hadn't returned home, and was still living with my parents. But now I began to see him regularly. A few months before Bill's miraculous transformation, in November of 1982 he had been arrested for illegal possession of a firearm, and selling liquor without a license. The after hours club that he had been working for as a bouncer had been raided by the police. And although he wasn't, he was charged as if he was the owner. The firearms charge alone carried a mandatory sentence of one year in jail. Bill was arraigned, remanded, and jailed at the Brooklyn Detention Center. However, his mother and I managed to post his bail. In March of 1983 Bill accompanied by his mother went to court. As he sat there, contemplating his fate, and waiting for the judge to enter the courtroom he heard a still small voice say to him "You're not going to jail." In that moment Bill suddenly knew that he wouldn't go lo jail, but he didn't know how that would come to pass. His lawyer asked the judge for a continuance, and was given a later date to come back to court. Bill left the court feeling elated, and told his mother that he wasn't going to jail. The last time Bill went to court, he and his mother went to the wrong courtroom. After they were in the courtroom, Bill suddenly realized that they were in the wrong courtroom. He jumped to his feet, grabbed his mother, and hurrying out into the hall, found the right court and as they were entering the room he heard his lawyer making a deal with the judge to sentence him to five years probation. That happened on August 19, 1983. Based on the words that he heard in the courtroom in March coming to pass, Bill went to church with Carol that Sunday, August 21, 1983. After his conversion he told me that when he went to church with Carol, he never intended to give his life to the LORD, he just wanted to express his gratitude.

The change in my husband was no less than phenomenal. I bought him a copy of the King James version of the Bible, and he immediately devoured it, reading whole books at a sitting. Because he had been arrested and his case fully adjudicated, he no longer had a job, and was able to stay home. He devoted himself to the LORD and read his Bible incessantly. I witnessed my husband fall completely in love with the LORD. My husband was truly a changed man. He had been using drugs and smoking both marujana and cigarettes for seventeen years. The LORD delivered him from his addictions in less than two weeks. Bill would spend hours on his knees, praying and reading the Book of Psalms. One evening while I was at my mother's house for our weekly Bible study, Bill called with some very exciting news. He had received the baptism of the Holy Spirit, and was speaking in what the Bible referred to as "others tongues." Everyone in the study rejoiced with him. After about a month or so, I went back home and began living life with my new husband. We went shopping for an entire bedroom suite, and we were loving our life together. However, it wasn't long before all hell broke loose in our lives once again. I still had some issues in my life that hadn't been dealt with, and I felt that my husband had become fanatical in his devotion to the LORD.

One evening as we were entertaining a neighbor who lived upstairs on the second floor, Bill and Bertha (our neighbor) began a conversation about my past and how I needed to be delivered from the effects of the abortions that I'd had. This provoked a violent reaction from me. I wasn't a violent person, nor had I ever lost my self control to anger. But as he continued trying to tell me what happened to me spiritually, before I realized what was happening to me, I hauled off and punched him in his mouth. I initially believed that I reacted like this, because unconsciously I was repressing some pent up anger. But later on I realized that I was wrong. I began to understand what really happened to me when my husband prayed for me and I began to manifest demonic oppression. My husband cast the demons of murder out of me, I began to experience a release from the demonic oppression that I had been suffering from for years.

Bill's family was completely caught off guard by his conversion. They weren't accustomed to him preaching to them, and most of them basically rejected him. Some of the older members of his family had always believed that he would never amount to anything. And now suddenly, here he was; one of the sons of the living God declaring the Gospel of Jesus Christ to them. His younger brother Dennis who was serving in the Air Force, and had become a Christian some years earlier was extremely happy for him. Dennis had been praying for his brother and myself for several years. Everywhere he went Bill would declare his testimony of how the LORD had kept him from going to jail, delivered him from drug addiction and filled him with the Holy Spirit. One day while preaching on 42nd street in midtown Manhattan, he met a young man named Bobby Coleman. Bobby gave him a portable speaker and microphone and they soon became fast friends. And together they went and preached the Gospel on the streets of Manhattan, Brooklyn, the Bronx, Queens, and on the trains of the New York transit system. Bill also preached the Gospel in our neighborhood park on Farragut Road in Flatbush Brooklyn. His old hangout buddies would see him and shout out to him "What's up Billy?" And he would exclaim in a booming voice; "JESUS CHRIST THE SON OF THE LIVING GOD!!!" That response would blow their minds, because it demonstrated the profound change that had taken place in his life They saw him go from dealing drugs to preaching the Gospel of Jesus Christ. Bill witnessed the Gospel to two of his cousins in Elizabeth, New Jersey who gave their lives to the LORD. He also ministered the Gospel in the Wall Street district of New York City, and many lives received the message and gave their lives to the LORD. It is because of his street ministry that many souls were saved.

During this period of our lives Bill wasn't working, and we couldn't keep up with all of our bills on my salary alone. This caused us to be evicted from our apartment once again, and we had to move back to my parent's home one more time. However, the LORD worked this out for our good. Spending our early days in salvation with my mother were some of the happiest days of our lives. Bill and my mother became very close, spending hours together talking about the LORD. There were times when I felt left out, but I soon realized that because of the spiritual bond that they developed they had formed a loving relationship, and Bill considered my mother to be not only his mother-in-law, but also his mother in the LORD. As for my mother, she was very happy to see my husband finally saved and delivered. After all, she had been praying for us for years, and now she was able to see her prayers come to fruition.

My mother invited us to do a street revival at Mother Cross's church on Church Avenue in Flatbush Brooklyn. My husband gave his testimony about how he had given his life to the LORD. Mother Cross had also invited other ministers to speak every night. After the revival meetings ended, Mother Cross invited Bill to assist her in conducting the services. She asked him to teach Sunday School, and to preach Sunday service every fourth Sunday morning.

As Bill began to minister the Word of God to the people on a regular basis, the church membership began to grow. Little did we realize that after a while, he was helping to pastor the congregation. Due to religious politics, things were out of order and there was an undercurrent of confusion in the ministry. However, remaining faithful to his calling. Bill continued to do the work. Every Saturday morning, Bill would go to the church building (a storefront) and spend his time studying the Word in order to get a message for God's people on Sunday morning. Bill also cleaned up the room where the services were held. I started missing my husband and said so to my mother. She chided me to leave him alone, because he was doing the work of the LORD. One Saturday after returning home from the building, Bill showed me something that the LORD had revealed to him in prayer. We had an address book that we used to write down all of our contact information. Bill opened that book and showed me something that he had written, "Cross of Calvary Deliverance Ministries." This was the title of the ministry that the LORD had given to him. After looking at it, we never spoke about it again. Bill also took over my mother's weekly Monday evening Bible study from Apostle Frank Dowtin. Apostle Dowtin had to leave the study for another assignment. This was the same minister who led the Bible study and who the LORD used to supernaturally influ-ence both myself and Sandra to give our lives to Him. Bill had a cousin named Alexis Bacourt who lived in Allentown Pennsylvania. Sometimes Alexis would come to my mother's house to visit us. We also would go to her house in Allentown, and spend the weekend with her. One Friday evening before leaving for Allentown, we went to my mother's church. I was on my cycle and experiencing terri-ble menstrual cramps and heavy bleeding during the service. I went downstairs to the restroom. While I was there, I felt this huge clot of blood come out of me. I nervously sent for Alexis, and when she got there, she examined what I had left in the toilet bowl and told me that I had a miscarriage. I was surprised, because I had no idea that I was pregnant and carrying our one and only child. It was sometime later before I told my husband that Alexis had informed me that we did have a child, but the baby didn't make it. I know that someday I will see all of the children that the LORD has blessed me with.

Bill met a lovely family who he introduced me to. Their names were Ronald and Caroline Pringle. They had five children, and they loved the LORD. Ronald often participated in our studies. One Monday evening he brought a minister with him. This minister operated in prophetic ministry. On this particular evening my sis-ter Joyce was visiting my mother. Joyce had been struggling with alcohol addiction, and some other issues for years, and she seemed to be restless. I had written her a four page letter telling her that she needed to change her life. As she sat there in my mother's beauty parlor, the man of God began speaking to her about everything that she was going through in her life. The minister spoke so accurately about what she was going through in her life that she recognized that the LORD was speaking to her through this man. Joyce was moved by the Holy Spirit, and gave up resisting the LORD. She surren-dered her life back to the LORD that night calling on His name. Her life instantly changed. All of us started praising God for Joyce. My mother was especially exuberant in her praise, because her prayers were being answered. Four of her children had given their lives to the LORD.

In the year 1985 my mother told me that the LORD had spoken to her and told her to go visit her youngest son Ronnie who lived in Richmond Virginia. My mother said she was to lead Ronnie to the LORD. Mother rented a van and her husband Otha drove me, my husband, my sister Joyce and her daughter Chauntele to see Ronnie. Ronnie lived in a housing complex on the southside of Richmond called the San Sousie apartments. His apartment was located on Clarkson Road. We arrived at Ronnie's apartment on Thanksgiving day. My brother had already cooked and prepared dinner for us.

As soon as we arrived my mother was suddenly stricken with a toothache. This was very strange, because she had never experienced a toothache before. We found a Patient First clinic and got her some pain medication. Pops also served to be a distraction. He took Ronnie out for drinks. And Ronnie had a lot of different girlfriends coming in and out of his apartment. We stayed with Ronnie from that Thursday until late Sunday afternoon. On Saturday Joyce and t went to the store, and on the way, we saw this beautiful apartment complex. It was resplendent with brand new beautiful townhouse apartments. We went to the rental office to inquire about them. I knew that we couldn't afford it, but I wanted to check them out anyway. The rental agent showed us the model apartment. It was equipped with two large bedrooms with two vanities in the master bedroom, a half bathroom downstairs, a mid-sized kitchen, a living room, dining room, and a patio. Our minds were completely blown when the rental agent told us that the apartment rented for only $380.00 a month. I immediately told my husband about It. He was excited and immediately wanted to see it for himself. We were still living with my parents, and needed our own place. But it was too expensive for us to live in Brooklyn at the time. We had planned to go back to Brooklyn that Sunday afternoon. However, before we left my mother insisted that my husband pray for Ronnie, because this was the main reason why she wanted to see him. When Bill prayed for him the anointing was so strong that the Holy Spirit literally arrested Ronnie and backed him up against his bedroom wall. We all rejoiced ecstatically when Ronnie repeated the Sinner's prayer. My mother's mission was accomplished. Through her diligent prayer and faith in God, another one of her children had given their life to the LORD. By the time we got back to Brooklyn, Ronnie had already begun reading the Bible that I had bought him some months earlier. We talked for hours on the phone, rejoicing and praising God for his salvation. I was never so happy for Ronnie.

Upon our arrival back to Brooklyn, I started making plans for us to move to Richmond Virginia. But getting into our new townhouse apartment wasn't going to be as easy as we hoped. Our goal was that we might acquire a two bedroom apartment. However, the rental agent insisted that we could only afford a one bedroom apartment. However, I continued to tenaciously insist that we needed a two bedroom apartment, and through prayer and the agency of the LORD, we prevailed. Bill had previously suggested that we get an extra bedroom just in case we needed to accommodate someone who might need our help. My mother was completely surprised by our decision to leave New York for Virginia. She didn't think that the LORD wanted us to move, but I explained to her that it was the LORD who opened this door, and Bill and I were embarking on this new journey together.

Bill and I in mutual agreement prayed for the LORD'S guidance and the LORD spoke Genesis 12:1 continually to his spirit for at least two weeks, letting him know that our decision to move was the right one. We made reservations to fly with Piedmont Airlines to Richmond Virginia on January 1st, 1986. We had a total savings amount of $700.00 that we spent in one day in order to acquire our apartment. My husband had to return to Brooklyn In order to work until he could find employment in Richmond.

Medical Personnel Pool, the nursing agency that I worked for in New York, was also located in Richmond. This allowed me to be able to find employment right away. I was able to get nursing home assignments that afforded me the ability to make money to pay the bills. Bill would also send me money orders from New York to pay the rent. It was very hard for us to be apart, but Bill would fly down to Richmond every other weekend. We also wrote to and called each other as much as possible.

Although Bill and I had rented our own apartment, while he continued to work in New York, I stayed with my brother Ronnie in his apartment. He became my close companion. He acquainted me with the neighborhood by driving me around to all the different grocery stores, and to several of my job assignments until I learned the bus routes and was able to take the bus. We also went to a local church together called Richmond Christian Center. On one particular Sunday after church service, Ronnie told me that I could no longer stay with him in his apartment. He boldly said to me "You're going to sleep in your own house tonight." I was fearful, but I knew that he was right. I had to get accustomed to living in my own home alone until my husband was able to join me permanently. Inevitably this turned out to be a good thing, because I was able to develop a closer relationship with the LORD through prayer and reading my Bible. We hadn't moved our furniture down yet, so my brother brought over a small mattress for me to sleep on and lent me a small television set. Everything was so peaceful and quiet that after a while, I was no longer afraid. When Bill came down on the weekends he would put in applications for a job. I did miss my mother and sister Joyce very much, but I would speak to my sister on the public phone at least once a week.

One day while I was visiting Ronnie, my husband called, and Ronnie told him that it was time for him to come home long before my husband stepped out on his faith and trusted the LORD to take care of us. We were still in the month of January, and it was snowing. The grocery stores were packed with people, because they were preparing to be shut in by the storm. I stayed home, because my husband was coming home for good that night. The LORD used a man named Lawyer Carter (no relation) who was a very good friend of my family to perform a labor of love that night. Lawyer used his van to transport all of our furniture to Richmond, and refused to allow us to pay him for it. He even refused to receive money for his gas. We will always remember him for that. When they arrived I was so happy to see my husband. The next morning I prepared a wonderful breakfast for him and our friend. And although there was a snowstorm Lawyer insisted on driving back to New York right after breakfast. I really enjoyed watching my husband getting accustomed to our new home. He put our bedroom and dining room sets together. We didn't have our living room suite yet, but we were finally together and very happy. We began to fellowship with Ronnie at his church. Before we left New York, my husband told me that the LORD had told him that someone was going to give him a car.

One Sunday while we were in church. a lady walked right up to my husband, and after learning that he had just moved here, offered to give him a car. We praised God for bringing His word to pass. Neither one of us knew how to drive, but Ronnie taught Bill, and Bill taught me. Our very first automobile was a 1968 Chevrolet Caprice Classic. My mother wasn't disappointed when we left, but she did cry, because she knew that we were starting a brand new life in Virginia. Ironically, I never imagined leaving my mother, and moving out of New York, but it was the LORD who had orchestrated this move, and it was good for us.

When my husband was unable to find any work, we began to be financially challenged. Both of us were constantly suffering from homesickness, and often wept bitterly. Prior to our leaving Brooklyn, Bill found a welding job making $15.00 an hour, but by then the LORD had led us to Richmond. So he had to leave that job. When he finally found another welding job in Richmond, he had to take a $10.00 an hour decrease in pay. In addition to that, he had to walk two miles to get to his job everyday. However, in spite of all of that, he was glad to be working again. Yes, we had some financial problems, but the LORD afforded us to overcome them.

In the year 1989 my husband celebrated his fortieth birthday. Ronnie and a few of his friends came over to celebrate Bill's birthday with him. However this wasn't a very good day for him, because having reflected upon his life, he felt as if he hadn't accomplished much. Ronnie cracked up laughing at him, but I reassured him that he'd accomplished a great deal in his life. I reminded him that in spite of everything he had gone through, he had given his life to the LORD and was now the man of God. I told him that he was a wonderful husband and provider. However, Ronnie never let him live down crying on his fortieth birthday.

LINDA CARTER

After a while we started a Bible study class in our dining area. At least five to ten people who wanted to study the Bible would attend the class. We taught the class every Monday evening. Several of the people repented and gave their lives to the LORD, and they were happy to be discipled in a way that they could understand what the Bible was teaching them. We attended several different church services in an attempt to discover just where the LORD wanted us to be. My husband received two invitations from two different pastors to teach their Sunday school classes. He accepted the position under Pastor James Moore. And under the anointing of the LORD he was able to establish a pretty good following for the class. Everyone would come to hear Minister Carter teach. He was an excellent teacher with an ability to explain the Word of God so plainly that even the children were able to understand it.

One weekend in 1988 we received a surprise visit from Apostle Frank Dowtin. He is the minister the LORD used to win myself and my friend Sandra to the LORD. He and his wife, along with a friend of theirs, spent a few hours with us telling us about his vision of starting a ministry in the Virginia Beach area.

Bill and I were very excited, because before we left Brooklyn, we had promised him that if he were to move to Virginia, we would be a part of his ministry. Not long after his initial visit, Apostle Dowtin called my husband to let him know that an ederly woman that he knew had given him a building In the Church Hill section of Richmond. Immediately my husband began helping Apostle Dowtin expedite his move to Richmond. At this particular time we were in fellowship with Pastor Jack Johnson. and his wife Mrs. Mary Johnson. This was a very lovely couple who had been very good to us. So, it was very difficult for us to tell them that we were leaving their ministry. However, we informed them that prior to us coming to them, we had made a promise to Apostle Dowtin, and they, in turn, released us.

During one of her visits In the summer of 1987, my mother prophesied to Bill and I that one of us was going to get a new job. Personally, I never thought that I would ever get a job in a hospital again, because before we left Brooklyn all nursing assistant jobs had been frozen. In spite of my trust in the LORD waning, I went to Chippenham Hospital to do an interview for a nursing assistant job anyway. To my shock and surprise, the interviewer told me that I had enough experience to be a registered nurse. In September of 1987, I started working at Chippenham Hospital on the sixth floor in their medical surgical unit as a nursing assistant.

During the month of February, 1988, my husband had to take me to the emergency room at Chippenham Hospital. The doctor told me that I had uterine fibroid tumors, and I needed to have surgery to remove them immediately. He said that my uterus resembled a six month old pregnancy. Believing God in prayer I went on with the surgery. However, there was a risk that I might have to have a hysterectomy. But, praise God, I woke up to see my husband standing over me with a huge grin on his face, and a picture of the fifteen tumors that the doctor had extracted from my womb. And, as a result of the surgery, I had to stay home for the next eight weeks recuperating, my darling husband waited on me hand and foot.

While I was recuperating from the surgery, Apostle Dowtin would stay with us for days at a time so that he could set up the ministry in Church Hill. My husband devoted his time to helping him, and we now considered him our pastor. Not long after completing my recuperation, and returning to work, I received a message informing me that my husband had fallen from the roof of the building in Church Hill, and had broken his left clavicle bone. By that time I had obtained my drivers license, and after finishing my shift was able to drive him home from the hospital. And, once again the LORD demonstrated His love for us by assigning a woman from the ministry to stay with us while my husband recuperated from his injury.

In the same way that he was there for me during my recuperation I was there for him during his. Because he wasn't able to use his arm, he needed my help bathing and dressing himself.

As we faithfully worked with Apostle Dowtin, we became the very first members of God's Deliverance Tabernacle. This is the name that the LORD gave to Apostle Dowtin for the ministry. My husband worked hard at building the membership of the church. Leading the soul-winning team he and his team knocked on many doors in the Church Hill community. They would set up home Bible studies with those who were interested. Many people gave their lives to the LORD, and became members of the fellowship. As the years passed, we suffered a lot of persecution, but the LORD saw us through it all. During this period of time two new ministers visited the fellowship. Their names were Inetta Hayward and Coleman Elliot. Both of these ministers were faculty members of Community Bible Institute, a Bible college located in Brooklyn, New York. Apostle Dowtin had invited them in for the purpose of building a school for the ministry. During their visit Dr. Hayward, who later became my husband's best friend, heard him teach, and liked what she heard. She became instrumental to my husband becoming a faculty member of the Community Bible Institute in Richmond. My husband who was now a licensed minister under the ministry of Apostle Dowtin, had an anointed ability to teach, and the people were confident that when they sat under his ministry they were going to learn their Bible. Minister Carter wasn't one to take shortcuts and didn't allow his students to do so. As a result many of the students thought him to be a tough teacher, nevertheless they knew him to be a great one. After a while Bill began to feel the anointing of evangelism. He talked to the Apostle, and got his permission to go forth as an evangelist. He evangelized the Gospel message in the urban and rural communities in and around the Richmond area. He went as far as Maryland and the surrounding areas preaching and teaching the Word of God. He also preached tent revivals and did prison ministry. I myself had also participated in women's prison ministry just before we left New York.

In November of 1986, on Thanksgiving Day morning my sister, Joyce Anne Odum went home to be with the LORD. This happened during the very same year that we moved to Richmond. Both Bill and myself were deeply saddened by her untimely death of lung cancer. Joyce was just thirty six years old when she passed. But before she passed, she became a true witness for the LORD. Although she was in perpetual pain, she evangelized all of her friends, and won her husband James to Christ. I was deeply hurt that the LORD had taken her so soon. Not only was Joyce my only living biological sister, she was also my best friend, and I just couldn't understand why the

LORD would take her so early. And It would take some more time before I would finally understand why she had to leave us. After we moved to Richmond, I would continue to call her, and she told me that she wanted to move here also. One day, during one of my calls to her she informed me that the doctors had discovered a spot on her lungs. At the time I didn't think about it very much. In fact, I thought she would eventually be healed from whatever they found.

Ironically, earlier that year, Joyce had asked for the entire family to come together for the Thanksgiving holiday. So, Bill and I rode to Brooklyn with a couple that had moved to Richmond from Queens, New York. We arrived at my parent's home in Brooklyn at 6:30am on Thanksgiving day. Our friend Sandra had invited us to go to sunrise service at her church. We decided to go with Sandra before going to visit Joyce, because Brooklyn Jewish Hospital, the hospital that she was in, had strict visitation rules. While we were in the service, we received a call from a family member informing us that Joyce had died. I couldn't believe what I was hearing, and when my husband heard it, he immediately started crying, and people began to gather around us in prayer. When we got back to my mother's house I was suddenly faced with the realization that I would never see my sister in the flesh again. As was stated earlier Joyce while being In perpetual pain and taking chemotherapy treatments had visited several of her friends and family members to tell them about Jesus, and His undying love for them. Joyce had also come to Richmont to witness our brother Ronnie get married. Joyce had lost most of her hair because of the chemo treatments. It was short and naturally curly. I would tease her and say, "This is the first time in our lives that your hair is shorter than mine," never realizing that she would never survive this devastating disease.

Everyone of the entire family experienced the loss of Joyce differently, but we all knew that she was with the LORD, and that one day we would all see her again. It took a long time for me to adjust to Joyce not physically being with us. It affected me to the point of not being able to sleep. Eventually I had to take sedatives in order to go to sleep. One day during this period, I was in the shower and the LORD gave me a new song called "When You've Lost the One you Love." I was very much comforted by this song.

One evening in 1994, while teaching a Bible class, my husband started talking about going forth in the ministry that the LORD called him to. Of course he told Apostle Dowtin about what the LORD was showing him. However, Apostle Dowtin and his wife were not happy for us at all. My husband and I were very disappointed. However, he knew that it was incumbent upon him to do what the LORD had called him to do. On that wonderful Sunday morning, April 24, 1994, Cross of Calvary Deliverance Ministries was born. And we had our first service at out townhouse apartment at 1616 Treehaven Drive Richmond, VA 23224. Our living room (which we called the Sanctuary) was soon filled with people praising and blessing the LORD. Later we both discovered how fickle people can be. Because as soon as they came they would also leave. Fortunately there was one person who faithfully participated in the ministry. His name is Richard Houchens. He and his daughter Ashley would faithfully attend service every Sunday. Now that Bill had taken on the work of pastoring, all hell broke loose in our lives. We both learned that doing ministry was daunting work. But through our faith in God we were able to continue doing the work. After about two years, Bill heard the LORD tell him to close the ministry and return to Capital Christian Deliverance Center. Apostle Dowtin hadn't given his blessing to him, so he had to return home in order to get it. This was a very humbling experience, but we went back to the Capital, and submitted ourselves and out one member to Apostle Dowtin. Just before we returned, we attended a five day convention that the Apostle had sponsored.

On that Friday, the first night of the return to the Capital, Apostle Dowtin asked my husband to speak. I should also mention that about a year before he moved his ministry to Blair Street, Apostle Dowtin had privately consecrated my husband to the office of the Apostle. So that when we returned to the Capital, Minister Carter returned as Apostle Carter. That night Apostle Carter preached a message called "Your Life is Ministry." Everyone in the sanctuary was blessed by this message. So much so that even Apostle Dowtin himself was blessed and exclaimed "Cross of Calvary Deliverance Ministries is You ministry!!!" And that was the acknowledgment that the LORD had sent him back to get. The public acknowledgment of my husband's ministry allowed me to resume singing with the praise team once again. After a few months faithfully working at the Capital, the LORD called us back to Cross of Calvary Deliverance Ministries. I had been telling my husband to ask the management office in our apartment complex to let us use the community center, to which the manager replied yes. We met with our pastor and told him that we had to leave again, and that the LORD had blessed us with the community center where we lived to have services.

As the years went by, my husband and I continued to grow closer in our love for and commitment to one another. In 1996, my husband extended his ministry to a radio broadcast called "Lift High the Cross Radio Broadcast." It was hosted on WFTH Faith Radio, a radio station owned and operated by Pastor Jack Johnson. We moved the ministry from our living room to the community center in the San Souci apartment complex. And I started a class for women called "Training the Woman of Man." Once again we were headed in the direction that the LORD has called us to go and complete the work. We are still learning and growing as we continue to perform our ministeriel services. And many people continue to be saved, healed, and delivered because of the proclamation and explanation of the Word of God. All of what the LORD has called us to do continues to contribute to many people going on to do greater works in the name of the LORD. Since our beginning, Cross of the Calvary Deliverance Ministries has been housed in several different locations, however, our vision remains the same. We continue to see people rescued from a life of sin and spiritual death, and to see people made completely whole even as we were.

The administration of our ministry has changed drastically. We no longer perceive our ministry through the eyes of religion. We now understand that life in service to the LORD is not performed through religious ritual, but rather is lived out in our everyday prac-tical experiences. With this new understanding, we now minister to people as the LORD places them in our path. We have been married forty five years, and both of us have come a mighty long way in both our martial, and our salvation experience since 1977. When we first began this journey together we had no idea of the greatness that God had intented for our lives. Our LORD and Savior, Jesus Christ has changed the direction of our lives from going to hell and changed our destination from eternal death to eternal life.

There were many times that we grew faint as we ran this race, and there were many times when we felt like quitting, and throwing in the towel. However, we learned that "winners never quit and quitters never win."

I pray that my story has encouraged you to know that the LORD is both the changer of minds and lives. I have never had another nervous breakdown or ever experienced mental illness again. Before receiving the LORD Jesus Christ in my life, the doctors had told both my husband and mother that I would never be the same again, and I am not. I am now a new creation in Christ Jesus.

This is a picture of me and my niece Chauntele,
whom I loved as a daughter.

My Hubby Bill and I, first year of marriage.

Our church wedding 8/27/77

My Pops giving me away.

So in love

My cousin Velma that I grew up with as teenagers.

Teenage years and living at home on 698 Sterling place.

Summer love 1976, when we first met

2 yrs of marriage

1st anniversary

Cross of Calvary Deliverance Ministries, founded
by my husband in 1994 in Richmond Va.

My beautiful mother
Mrs Maggie Melissa Hall Jones

My family: Brother Aaron, David Ronnie, me, my parents
Maggie & Aaron Hall, sister Joyce, Rosemary and Vernon.

698 Sterling place, the home that I grew up
in as a teenager and young adult.

Graduated HS

The beginning of my depression

Me and Mom on her 80th Birthday

My sister Joyce and I when I lived
at 1414 New York ave

CPSIA information can be obtained
at www.ICGtesting.com
Printed in the USA
BVHW051644060922
646327BV00016B/100